auténtica cocina de españa

authentic spanish cooking

Betty A. Blue

A SPECTRUM BOOK

PRENTICE-HALL, INC., Englewood Cliffs, New Jersey 07632

Library of Congress Cataloging in Publication Data

BLUE, BETTY A.
    Authentic Spanish cooking = Auténtica cocina de
España.

    (Creative cooking series) (A Spectrum Book)
    Includes index.
    1. Cookery, Spanish.   I. Title.   II. Title:
Auténtica cocina de España.   III. Series.
TX723.5.S7B57   641.5946   81-5870
                                          AACR2

ISBN 0-13-054080-3

ISBN 0-13-054072-2 {PBK.}

10 9 8 7 6 5 4 3 2 1

Editorial/production supervision by Carol Smith
Cover design by Honi Werner
Chapter-opening art by Andrea S. Booth
Manufacturing buyer: Cathie Lenard

PRENTICE-HALL INTERNATIONAL, INC., London

PRENTICE-HALL OF AUSTRALIA PTY. LIMITED, Sydney

PRENTICE-HALL OF CANADA, LTD., Toronto

PRENTICE-HALL OF INDIA PRIVATE LIMITED, New Delhi

PRENTICE-HALL OF JAPAN, INC., Tokyo

PRENTICE-HALL OF SOUTHEAST ASIA PTE. LTD., Singapore

WHITEHALL BOOKS LIMITED, Wellington, New Zealand

To Robert Todd,
Erin Michelle, and Melissa Michelle

The creative cooking series
Every recipe in each of our cookbooks has been
kitchen tested by the author.

contents

preface

Several years ago, I was fortunate enough to be awarded a Fulbright-Hayes scholarship to Spain. Part of the cultural aspect of this program was traveling to all parts of the Iberian Peninsula and, of course, enjoying the cuisine. I had always had the mistaken idea that Spanish cooking resembled Mexican cooking. When I saw TORTILLAS on menus everywhere, I naturally assumed that these were the flat corn-type pancake served with every meal in Mexico. Instead, "tortillas" in Spain turned out to be omelets that are original and delicious. On that first trip, I was delighted to discover the many other culinary pleasures that this beautiful country offers, and I have collected recipes on my subsequent visits.

Spanish cooking became widely known in the United States in the 1960s during and after the New York World's Fair, as the Spanish Pavilion was one of the main attractions. A number of res-

taurants were opened in New York City at that time featuring Spanish cuisine, and these restaurants are still popular.

I have been asked how I could use AUTHENTIC in the title for AUTHENTIC MEXICAN COOKING (Englewood Cliffs, N.J.: Prentice-Hall, Inc. 1977) and now AUTHENTIC SPANISH COOKING. Common synonyms are VALID, BONA FIDE, GENUINE, and REAL. So I shall say that these are genuine recipes collected in Spain, converted from the metric system, and utilize ingredients readily available in the supermarkets in the United States.

Other interesting titles might have been EATING YOUR WAY TO HEALTH, EATING YOURSELF THIN, or even EATING FOR BEAUTY. These titles are also fundamentally authentic, for both olive oil and garlic in the diet are considered health foods. Spanish children are the most beautiful, healthy-looking youngsters I have ever seen. Spaniards eat at least one multicourse meal a day, but they eat slowly over a period of a couple of hours. The average Spaniard does not look like the emaciated Don Quixote, nor does he resemble the obese Sancho Panza. Spanish food looks appetizing, for it is colorful and served beautifully. The tendency of the American would be to overeat, but I can honestly say that I have always lost weight in Spain. As for beauty, look at the complexion of the Spanish woman, and you will see another value of olive oil.

la cultura y la cocina de españa

1

spanish culture and cuisine

The saying "You are what you eat" may very well be true. However, the cuisine of Spain is especially reflected in its history and its geography. No other country in the world has been the locale of so many foreign invasions, nor is any other country in Europe, with the exception of Switzerland, as mountainous, thus making the various regions of the Peninsula diversified and differentiating the inhabitants from one another.

The Iberian Peninsula is the remainder of a continental territory originally connected to Africa by Gibralter. It is a complete geographic entity, surrounded by seas on all sides for some 88 percent of its periphery, except to the northwest where the tall Pyrenees Mountains separate Spain from France. Thus, we can readily understand why fish is an important part of the diet. The Spanish territory covers some 85 percent of the Iberian Peninsula, with Portugal, located to the west of Spain, occupying the remaining 15 percent.

EARLY INHABITANTS From antiquity, the Peninsula has acted as a bridge between the African and European continents, frequently being invaded from the north by people in search of new booty and those from Africa who fell in love with the "paradise of the gods" opposite their lands. The result was a mixture of the races and cultures, and the cultures included the cuisines. This mixture of

2

peoples and civilizations through the centuries has given the race and culture of the Iberian Peninsula special peculiarities, different from the general ones in Europe.

THE PHOENICIANS. The Phoenicians were the first of the eastern Mediterranean people known to have voyaged to the Iberian Peninsula, where they settled in Gadir (present-day Cádiz) around 1100 BC. Although these traders were attracted to this southwestern portion of the country by the mineral wealth, they established a series of fisheries and factories for salting fish. This introduction to fish preservation was the origin of the vast fish industry in Spain.

The name SPAIN also has been attributed to the Phoenicians, being derived from I-SAPHAN-IM, which means coast or island of the rabbits. This animal was unknown to the Phoenicians but was abundant on the Peninsula. Today delicious rabbit dishes are still available in Spain.

THE GREEKS. The Greeks were commercial rivals of the Phoenicians from a very early age. The Greeks arrived in the southern part of the Peninsula (Tartessos) during the seventh century before Christ, having been diverted from their course toward Egypt by a storm. Here they founded the celebrated colony of Emporion, today known as Ampurias, located on the coast of Catalonia. They did not penetrate the interior, for neither the Phoenicians nor the Greeks had a conquering spirit.

The civilizing influence of the Greeks is evident. They brought to the primitive inhabitants of the Peninsula commerce, industry, and agriculture. The Greeks introduced the cultivation of grapes and olives. What would Spain be today without its marvelous grape wines, olives, and the olive oil business? It is the largest producer of olive oil in the world; the marvelous climate and the brilliant

3

sunshine make the olive oil produced in Spain superior in quality to that produced anywhere else.

THE CARTHAGINIANS. During the sixth century before Christ, the Carthaginians, a people of Phoenician origin, arrived in Spain supposedly to aid the Phoenicians against some native tribes who were revolting. This provided the excuse for the inevitable expansion of the Carthaginian power, as the helpers became the dominators. The Carthaginians were driven from the Peninsula by the Romans at the end of the Second Punic War in 201 BC.

THE CELTS. The Celts, a pagan people, originated from central Europe. They believed in the powers of plants and animals. It is possible that they first arrived in Iberia from northern France and from the Rhine region as early as 700 BC and continued their invasions for several centuries.

The Celts settled in three different areas of the Peninsula but left their greatest influence to the north of the valley of the Duero, where they established important towns in the provinces of Asturias and Pontevedra in Spain and Briteiros in Portugal. Even today, the cooking strongly reflects the history of that region.

THE CELTIBERIANS. The Celtiberians were a mixture of the Celts and the Iberians. The term originated with the Romans who used it to describe the ancient Spanish population. Whether these primitive people were the result of a mixture or not, it is certain that the Iberian element was the dominant one, as they were stronger and more civilized than the Celts. Indeed, while the Iberians were profiting from the influence of the Mediterranean civilizations, the Celts were still in the prehistoric level of the Age of Iron.

THE IBERIANS. Greek navigators gave the name IBERIAN to the ancient population who originally lived around the Iberus (now called Ebro) River. It is believed that the Iberians may have migrated from northern Africa. The figure of the Iberian is the typically small, dark Mediterranean type in contrast with the Nordic appearance found in predominantly Celtic locations of the Peninsula. We know that in the sixth century BC, they occupied the south and east of Spain.

THE ROMANS. The original Roman invasion of Spain in 218 BC had the objective of isolating the Carthaginian general, Hannibal, from his supply bases. However, the many riches found on the Peninsula, not only in mineral wealth but also in manpower, brought about the conquest.

It was the Romans who adopted the name Hispania for all of the Peninsula, including Portugal. The great Roman contribution to the Peninsula was the founding of the basis of a nation with one government, one law, one language, and a common culture.

Although the Romans exploited the great riches of the mines, livestock, agriculture, and fishing of the Peninsula, there was the added advantage of all the technical advancements which the Romans brought to Spain. The Romans furthered the growth of olive trees and introduced garlic to the Peninsula. When we think of a typically Spanish dish today, it always contains olive oil and garlic.

Of special interest for the future agricultural growth of Spain was DE RE RUSTICA by the Hispanic Lucius Junius Moderatus Columela. Written in twelve books, it is the most complete treatise on agriculture in ancient times. The subjects of the first nine books are general precepts—land and crops, vineyards, trees, land dimensions, and live-

stock, in which Columela included birds, bees, and fish. His tenth book was devoted entirely to gardening. His eleventh volume was on the duties of an overseer of an estate or farm. This book included the work that must be done during each month of the year and cultivation of gardens and garden herbs. Columela's works were based on his personal experiences more than on existing theories and give us insight into the agricultural activity of the first century AD in Spain.

THE VISIGOTHS. The first invasion by the Vandals, the Alanis, and the Suevians in 409 AD did not have a permanent character. The Vandals settled for a time in a great part of southern Spain that they called Vandalusia (now Andalusia). The Alanis settled in Lusitania (now Portugal). From these Germanic people, only the Suevians, who settled in the region least Romanized, Galicia, were of a more lasting nature until they were absorbed by the Visigoth monarchy a century and a half later.

The Gothic domination was different from all of the previous ones, for it was not a colonial conquest but the mass immigration of a whole people to another territory. Here they conserved their racial identity, their customs, and their beliefs. They prohibited mixed marriages between Goths and Spanish-Romans.

The Visigoth idea of a monarchy was based on the Roman tradition even to the point of the adoption of the title "Emperor" by some of the kings. This intense Romanization of the Visigoths suffered from the corruption of some of the political vices of the decadent Empire. The dynamic rivalries and intense wars weakened the Visigoth monarchy; personal and partisan interests took precedence over the national interest. Thus, the Visigoth kingdom fell easily in the face of Arab attacks.

6

SPANISH MOSLEMS. Except for a small number of Visigoths who took refuge in Asturias, the cities of the Peninsula were subdued by the Moslem invaders nearly without resistance beginning in 711 AD. Although the Arabs conquered Spain in some seven years, it was going to take the Spanish-Christians more than seven hundred years to reconquer it completely.

The Moslems were generally called MOORS in Spain. The term ARABS should rightly belong to those Moslems born in Arabia, while the term MOORS should refer to the inhabitants from Morocco, who did form the majority of those coming to Spain.

Mixed marriages were common not only among the lower classes but also among the very highest classes, even the nobility. The majority of these marriages involved Arabic men and Christian women, for the occupation force, unlike the previous Gothic invaders, involved some 30,000 men who did not bring their families.

It was in the southern part of the Peninsula, called Al-Andalus (now Andalusia) where the Arabs finally were to settle for over seven hundred years. A large number of Spanish-Christians continued to live in Moslem territory. This group was so numerous that they received the special name of MOZÁRABES, which means "Arab Hangers-on" or "Would-be Arabs." These people were the principal means of bringing the Arab influence into Christian Spain.

Between the eighth and twelfth centuries, the Arabs dominated the world. The Arabic language was spoken from India to Spain. During the tenth century, Cordova, the capital of the caliphate, became the principal intellectual center of the western world, while London and Paris were still two insignificant cities. The capital city was trans-

7

formed into a majestic court of Oriental splendor, with paved streets, hundreds of mosques, luxurious palaces and gardens, public baths, and excellent private libraries.

Through a process of gradual emancipation, the Christian states were expanding and uniting until there were three principal ones on the Peninsula: Castile in the center (the conqueror of the greatest amount of territory), Aragon-Catalonia in the east, and Portugal in the west. The strength of the Christian states was increased greatly by the marriage of Ferdinand of Aragon and Isabella of Castile and ultimately brought about the fall of Granada, the last Moorish stronghold, in the early days of 1492.

CULTURAL INFLUENCES ON CUISINE   Early inhabitants of the Peninsula were very influential in introducing the current cuisine in Spain.

To the Phoenicians the Spanish owe the fisheries and the means of preserving fish, which was unknown to the native inhabitants. Today fresh fish is available in every part of the Iberian Peninsula, even in Madrid, the center of Spain.

The Greeks brought the first olive trees and probably grapevines. The Greek women used olive oil as an excellent cosmetic for the care of the skin; today it is used in a great variety of dermatological preparations. However, even during the time of the Greeks, olives and olive oil were used for human consumption.

Whether the Phoenicians or the Greeks brought the first grapevines to the Peninsula, the wine of Spain has been prized since ancient times. The finest wine in the world today is still produced where the original grapevines were planted in the southernmost tip of Spain. The province is called Cádiz, and the town is Jerez de la Frontera, named

by the Christian natives after the invaders had been driven from the land. When one orders JEREZ in Spain, one is ordering a dry sherry.

When in Spain, you must visit a BODEGA (wine factory). I was very impressed with the cleanliness everywhere, and the grounds outside the factory were breathtakingly beautiful. By the time you leave a BODEGA, you may think it was the best time you've ever had in your life, for the guides are very generous with the samples.

The provinces of Galicia and Asturias in the northwest corner of Spain were strongly influenced by the Celts, who settled in that area with their families. The cuisine strongly reflects the history of the region. When we think of Asturias, we automatically picture FABADA ASTURIANA, a type of bean stew made famous in that area. Galicia is the home of the EMPANADA, a pie made of meat or seafood that is usually served cold.

If we credit the Greeks or perhaps even the Phoenicians with bringing the first olive trees to the Peninsula, we must give the Romans credit for their technical advancements in agriculture. In ancient times olive trees were first known in the countries of the eastern Mediterranean, but the warm Spanish sun and the soil conditions proved ideal for their cultivation, thus making the olive oil produced there superior in quality to that produced elsewhere. It is interesting to note that the word OIL in the Latin language specifically meant olive oil.

The olive is technically a fruit rather than a vegetable, although olive oil is generally included in the same category as vegetable oils. There are many varieties of olive trees grown in all areas of Spain today making that country by far the world leader in olive-oil production.

Olive oil is the only oil that can be used in its pure, unrefined state. It has been called the king of edible fats. There are many grades of olive oil, and one can get bad oil even in Spain. The highest quality is that which comes from the first pressing. This virgin oil will also remain fresh on your kitchen shelf for the longest time. Olive oil should not be refrigerated, since any change in flavor is caused by impurities in the oil rather than by heat.

Olive oil does not contain cholesterol. It is low in saturated fat, high in unsaturated fat, and it has no additives. The heart is a muscle and needs a number of energy-giving foods: one of these is oleic acid, and olive oil has more of this than any other food. Contrary to what many believe, scientific studies have proved that olive oil does not in any way bring about an increase in weight.

The Romans also brought garlic to the Peninsula. Before the discovery of America and the introduction of tobacco to Europe, the Spanish soldiers would chew raw garlic to give them courage before they went into battle. Later, tobacco was substituted for the garlic. Today it would be virtually impossible to have a meal in Spain without garlic, but it is added so subtly that the diner is not aware of it.

I shall never forget my first trip to Spain some years ago when Generalísimo Franco was at the height of his power. I noticed that everyone I met smelled of garlic; it took me several months to realize that I smelled the same way.

Of all the early invaders of the Peninsula, perhaps none have influenced the cuisine as much as the Moslems. Spices must be considered the greatest innovation of the Arabs to the people of the Peninsula. The diet was monotonous and unpalatable. Food spoiled quickly. Spices served the dual purpose of adding flavor to otherwise flavorless food

10

and, in the case of some spices, inhibiting spoilage.

Spices were the most valued commodities in the ancient trade centers. They were in short supply and very expensive; for example, pepper was sold by the individual peppercorn. The camel caravans that carried these treasures originated in southern India and ran through long, torturous routes via Afghanistan, Persia, Syria, Arabia, across the Red Sea into Egypt, and then to Arabian ports. Because these caravans were mostly owned and operated by Arabs, they monopolized the spice trade for hundreds of years. When they invaded the Peninsula in the year 711 AD, they probably knew more about herbs and spices than any other civilization. Some of the spices still used in Spain today that were brought by the Moslems include basil, cinnamon, cloves, ginger, nutmeg, and pepper.

It was the Arabs who introduced some extremely important agricultural products, such as rice, cotton, sugar cane, oranges, lemons, apricots, spinach, artichokes, and even nuts. Even a great number of current Spanish words, the majority of which are agricultural products and start with the letter A, originated from the Arabic: for example, ALGODÓN (cotton), ALBARICOQUE (apricot), ARROZ (rice), ALCACHOFA (artichoke), AZAFRÁN (saffron), AZUCAR (sugar), ESPINACA (spinach), and COMINO (cumin).

One of the most popular dishes in all of Spain today is GAZPACHO, which originated in Andalusia but was directly descended from Arabic cookery. Because of the hot climate of southern Spain, GAZPACHO, a tomato-based soup served cold, has to be a favorite. Although each cook may have his or her own way of preparing this soup, the basic ingredients are the same: chopped tomatoes, garlic, fine olive oil, and wine vinegar ground together

with day-old bread. The modern cook in Spain has an electric blender and will blend the ingredients together. Water is added and the mixture is refrigerated to settle and chill. It is served with side dishes of chopped cucumber, tomatoes, bell pepper, and croutons.

The last Moorish stronghold, Granada, fell in 1492. It is no coincidence that this is also the date of the discovery of America, for Columbus was looking for another route to the Far East in order to ensure that the spice trade would not be stopped after the Moors were no longer in Spain.

SPANISH MEALS   The hours when Spaniards eat and the five meals that they have each day are a great mystery to Americans. The day begins rather early with DESAYUNO, which means breakfast but is not what Americans think of as breakfast. It consists of coffee or chocolate and rolls. Around 11:00 in the morning the natives have ALMUERZO, which translates as lunch but may be a more substantial breakfast with eggs and sausage or perhaps appetizers served with wine or beer.

The multi-course meal served between 2:00 and 3:00 in the afternoon called the COMIDA begins with either ENTREMESES (side dishes of olives, pickles, etc.), soup, or a salad. The salad will probably be lettuce and tomatoes with an olive oil and vinegar dressing. The soup may well be SOPA DE AJO, a garlic soup characteristic of all the provinces and prepared in a number of different ways. The main course will be fish, meat, or game. For dessert, one may be served fresh fruit or flan, which is the national dessert of Spain and is a type of caramel custard. Although wine is served with the meal, coffee is not served until after the dessert course. As the stores and offices close for three hours in the afternoon, Spaniards habitually take a siesta (nap) after this substantial repast.

Around 6:00 it is time for the MERIENDA (which means afternoon refreshments). This may be coffee and pastries; or one may prefer to bar hop, strolling leisurely from one sidewalk café to another, stopping for a glass of wine and TAPAS.

The night meal called the CENA really is at night, being served between 10:00 and midnight. In Madrid many restaurants do not even open until 10:00 PM. When one is dining at home, this will be more like the ALMUERZO or MERIENDA, a very light meal of soup and an omelet or perhaps a fish dish. However, if this is an occasion with guests or if one is dining in a restaurant, a multi-course meal like the COMIDA will again by enjoyed.

los aperitivos

2

appetizers

TYPES OF APPETIZERS   Although the Spanish word TAPA means a cover or a lid, in Spain TAPAS are appetizers served in restaurants, sidewalk cafés, and bars during the late afternoon and evening. They may be relatively simple like toasted almonds or olives, both of which are native to Spain, or they may be canapés of shrimp, herring, salmon, smoked eel, foie-gras, ham, duck, chicken, or cheese requiring hours to prepare.

As the evening shadows begin to fall, the natives leave their homes to stroll up and down the streets. To encourage this promenade, blocks are closed to motorized traffic, even in the cities. Along these streets are masses of strollers of all ages, especially young men and women carrying babies in their arms or pushing carriages. As night falls, the crowd becomes greater, and the sidewalk cafés or bars that line the streets are filled to capacity. Here one may enjoy drinks such as Jerez (a dry sherry from Jerez) and take advantage of the TAPAS, which are always served at that hour.

CANAPÉS.   Savory appetizers using day-old bread as a base cut in bite-size circles, diamonds, squares, or other shapes and deep fat fried in olive oil are canapés. Garnish each fried piece of bread with a number of spreads. Remember not to rush with the preparation of canapés, for they should be attractive.

EMPAREDADOS. Bite-size sandwiches with crusts removed and cut in triangles or rectangles are emparedados. Normally the spread is mayonnaise and the filling is ham or cheese, or both. Emparedados may be served hot or cold.

MEDIAS NOCHES. Although MEDIAS NOCHES translates into English as midnight snacks, in Spain the custom is not reserved for the midnight hour. When I think of MEDIAS NOCHES, I visualize a bite-size canapé served on a small buttered roll, rather than bread, and filled with thin slices of meat, usually ham.

TARTALETAS. These are tart shells which may be prepared a couple of days in advance and stored in a bread box or other metal container. They may be round or oblong like little boats depending on the filling. The shells should not be stuffed until just before serving. The recipe for tart shells follows.

Masa quebrada por tartaletas

Dough for Tart Shells

1 1/2 cups self-rising flour · 1 teaspoon salt · 1 egg · 2 tablespoons olive oil · cold water, about 4 tablespoons ·

In a large bowl, mix the salt in the flour. Add egg and olive oil; mix well with fingers.

Add the water a tablespoon at a time until the dough can be kneaded into a ball. Do not handle any more than is necessary or the dough will be tough. Cover with a damp cloth and set aside for 30 minutes.

Roll out on a lightly floured board until about 1/8 inch thick. Cut into 20 portions and place in lightly greased muffin tins or form in the shape of little boats. Pierce bottom several places with a fork.

Preheat oven to 400° and bake about ten minutes or until lightly browned. If using muffin tins or molds

17

remove immediately. Allow the shells to cool before storing.

MAKES 20 TART SHELLS.

Tartaletas may be filled with a variety of delicacies. It is best to wait until serving to fill the shells. Here are a few suggestions, but you may be able to think of something much more original.

Tartaletas de atún

Tuna Tarts

6 1/2 ounce can tuna, drained · 2 tablespoons mayonnaise · green pimiento-style olives, for garnish ·

Mix the tuna with the mayonnaise. Fill the shells and garnish with the olives sliced very thin with the pimiento in the center.

MAKES 1 CUP OF FILLING.

Tartaletas de salmón ahumado

Smoked Salmon Tarts

1 cup smoked salmon, well-drained if canned · 1 tablespoon lemon juice · 1 tablespoon onion, grated · butter ·

Mix the salmon with the lemon juice and onion. Butter the shells; fill with the salmon mixture and serve.

MAKES 1 CUP OF FILLING.

Tartaletas de jamón y piña

Ham and Pineapple Tarts

butter · 1 cup
cooked ham,
chopped, or ham
salad · pineapple
pieces,
well-drained ·
grated Cheddar
cheese, for topping ·

Butter the tartaletas and fill with the cooked ham or ham salad. I prefer the ham salad. Top each tartaleta with one piece of pineapple covered with grated cheese. Heat at 325° for 5 minutes before serving.

MAKES 1 CUP OF FILLING.

Tartaletas de caviar

Caviar Tarts

1/2 cup of caviar ·
4 hard-boiled eggs,
finely chopped ·
1 lemon · butter ·
pimiento, for
garnish ·

Mix the caviar with the eggs and the juice of 1 lemon. If the lemon is room temperature, it will yield more juice. Butter the tartaletas; fill; garnish with a small piece of pimiento and serve.

MAKES 1 CUP OF FILLING.

Barquitas de gambas

Shrimp Boats

1/2 cup mayonnaise ·
3 tablespoons
horseradish ·
1 teaspoon lemon
juice · 1/2 pound
shrimp, cooked or
canned · parsley,
for garnish ·

Use the boat-shaped shells, if possible. Mix the mayonnaise, horseradish and lemon juice together. Spread each shell with this mixture; then fill the shells with several shrimp depending on their size. Garnish each with a small piece of parsley. Serve chilled.

MAKES 20 TARTS.

Tartaletas de champiñon

Mushroom Tarts

1/2 cup butter ·
juice of 1/2 lemon ·
1/2 pound
mushrooms, finely
chopped ·

FOR THE SAUCE:
1/2 cup butter ·
1 tablespoon olive
oil · 2 tablespoons
flour · 1/2 teaspoon
salt · 1 cup cold
milk · 1/2 teaspoon
curry powder ·
parsley ·

Melt the butter in a skillet with the lemon juice. Add the mushrooms and simmer about 5-8 minutes.

In a separate small frying pan, prepare the sauce by melting the butter and oil. Add the flour and salt; stir with a wooden spoon until well blended. Remove from the heat and gradually stir in the milk until the mixture is smooth. Continue to stir over very low heat for some five minutes until smooth and thick. Add the curry powder and mix in the skillet with the mushrooms.

Fill the tart shells, garnish with parsley and serve hot.

MAKES 20 TARTS.

Tartaletas de Béchamel

Béchamel Sauce Tarts

3 tablespoons
butter ·
3 tablespoons
flour · 1 cup milk ·
1/2 cup light cream ·
nutmeg, few
grains · 1 teaspoon
salt · black or white
pepper, few grains ·
1 egg yolk, beaten ·
1/2 cup sharp
Cheddar cheese,
grated ·

Melt the butter over very low heat and stir in the flour until it begins to brown. Gradually stir in the milk with a wooden spoon. Be sure the sauce remains smooth.

Gradually add the cream and seasoning, stirring until thick and smooth. Stir in the egg yolk and cheese.

Fill the tarts and serve hot, or heat in a 325° oven for five minutes.

MAKES 1 1/2 CUPS.

Any of the fillings for TARTALETAS can be used for canapé spreads served on toasted or deep fat fried day-old bread cut in bite-size circles, diamonds, squares, or other shapes. Cocktail crackers of many shapes and varieties may be used as the base for any of the following recipes.

One cup of spread should cover from 25 to 35 small canapés.

Caviar de berenjena

Eggplant Caviar

2 medium eggplants · 1 cup water · 1 cup canned tomatoes, drained · 1 tablespoon tomato paste · 1 clove garlic, crushed · 1 teaspoon lemon juice · 1 teaspoon vinegar · 1/4 cup olive oil · 1 tablespoon capers · Tabasco, few drops · 1 tablespoon onion, minced · 1 teaspoon sugar ·

Peel and slice eggplant. Cook in 1 cup water until tender. Drain and mash. Add remaining ingredients and mix well. Chill several hours or overnight. Serve as spread for bread or crackers.

MAKES 2 1/3 CUPS.

Canapés de mayonesa y queso, calientes

Mayonnaise and Cheese Canapés, Served Hot

4 ounce package cream cheese, room temperature · 1/2 cup thick mayonnaise · 1/2 loaf day-old bread · onion, small slices ·

Thoroughly cream the cheese and mayonnaise together. (see page 26 for Spanish mayonnaise recipe if you are preparing your own.)

Cut the bread in round canapés about the size of half dollars. Spread each with the cheese-mayonnaise mixture and top with a small slice of onion.

Bake in a 325° oven until brown, being careful not to burn them. Serve hot.

Canapés de queso, tomate y bacón

Cheese, Tomato, and Bacon Canapés

Remove the crusts from day-old bread; sliced in half. Spread the halves lightly with soft butter. On each piece of bread place a slice of sharp Cheddar cheese. Top the cheese with a very thin slice of a well-ripened tomato. Place a piece of bacon over the tomato. You may prefer to partially fry the bacon first.

Bake in a 325° oven until the cheese melts and the bacon is done. Serve hot.

Canapés de queso Gervais y pimentón

Cheese and Paprika Canapés

Remove the crusts from day-old square bread, and cut each piece in fourths. Place a thick slice of Gruyére or Romano cheese on each piece. Sprinkle with a little salt and paprika.

Bake in a 300° oven until the cheese begins to melt. Serve hot.

Emparedados de queso blanco

White Cheese (bite-size) Sandwiches

1 cup Whey, Monterey Jack or mild Cheddar cheese, grated ·
2 tablespoons evaporated milk, unsweetened ·
1 tablespoon onion, finely chopped · 6 slices dark rye bread ·

The white cheese or "queso blanco" of Spain cannot be exactly duplicated in the United States.

Combine the grated cheese with the milk and onion. Add more milk if the mixture seems too thick to spread.

Remove the crusts from the bread and cut each slice in fourths. Spread the mixture and make the sandwiches. Refrigerate several hours before serving.

MAKES 24 OPEN-FACED SANDWICHES.

Palitos fritos de queso

Fried Cheese "Palitos"

1/2 cup parmesan cheese, grated · 1/2 cup flour · 1 tablespoon soft butter · 1 egg, separated · 1/4 teaspoon salt · olive oil ·

Combine cheese, flour, butter, egg yolk and salt. Fold in the egg white, beaten to a peak.

Roll out on a lightly floured board until about 1/2 inch thick. Cut in strips about 2 inches long or shape into balls about 1 inch in diameter.

Deep fat fry in olive oil at 375° until a golden brown. May be served hot or cold.

MAKES ABOUT 24 APPETIZERS.

Palitos de queso al horno

Baked Cheese "Palitos"

1/2 cup butter · 3 tablespoons flour · 1/2 cup sharp Cheddar cheese, grated · salt, to taste · 1 cup bread crumbs ·

Melt the butter over very low heat being careful that it does not burn. Remove from the heat. Add the flour, then the cheese and salt.

Mold the "palitos" into oblong shapes about 1/2 inch thick and 3 inches long.

Put the bread crumbs on a plate and dip each "palito" in the crumbs; then place on a cookie sheet.

Bake at 325° until the "palitos" are brown. Remove them from the pan very carefully, as they are fragile. Cool before serving.

MAKES ABOUT 24 "PALITOS."

Apio con roquefort

Celery Stuffed with Roquefort

Wash the celery stalks; drain on paper towels. Cut in 2-inch slices.

Mix equal parts of softened Roquefort cheese and butter. Fill the celery slices with this mixture. Refrigerate for several hours and serve cold.

Olivas de ajo

Garlic Olives

1 (3 ounce) jar pimiento-stuffed olives · 1 (5 3/4 ounce) can black olives, pitted · 1 cup olive oil · 4 cloves garlic, crushed · 2 tablespoons vinegar ·

Combine ingredients in a glass jar. Cover and refrigerate. Let stand 24 hours or more before serving.

SERVES 6-8.

Bocados de pollo

Chicken Bites

3 whole chicken breasts, split, boned and skinned · 1 egg, beaten · 1 teaspoon salt · 1/4 teaspoon pepper · 1 cup seasoned bread crumbs · 1/2 cup olive oil ·

Cut chicken into about 35 bite-size pieces. Mix egg, salt, pepper. Dip chicken pieces into egg mixture. Coat with crumbs. Heat olive oil in large skillet; sauté chicken until brown on both sides. Serve immediately on toothpicks.

MAKES 6 TO 8 SERVINGS.

Tostado de gambas

Shrimp Toast

In recent years, a large Oriental influx to the Iberian Peninsula has influenced the cuisine. I have enjoyed these shrimp hors d'oeuvres many times in Spain and hope you will too.

1/2 pound uncooked shrimp · 6 water chestnuts, finely chopped · 1 egg, slightly beaten · 1 teaspoon salt · 1 teaspoon sherry · 1/2 teaspoon ground ginger · 1 tablespoon scallion or onion, chopped · 1/2 tablespoon sugar · 1 tablespoon cornstarch · 8 slices white bread · 2 cups olive oil ·

Clean and chop shrimp. Mix with water chestnuts, egg, salt, sherry, ginger, scallion, sugar, and cornstarch. Trim crusts from bread. Cut each slice into quarters. Spread 1 heaping tablespoon of shrimp mixture over each quarter of bread,

Heat oil to 375° in small saucepan. Deep fry with shrimp side down for about 30 seconds. Turn over; fry for 5 seconds until the bread is slightly browned. Drain.

MAKES 32 HORS D'OEUVRES.

Mayonesa española

Spanish Mayonnaise

2 egg yolks · 1 teaspoon salt · 1/2 teaspoon dry mustard · 1 cup olive oil · 1 tablespoon vinegar (or 1/2 tablespoon lemon juice) ·

Mix the egg yolks, salt, and mustard in an electric mixer or blender at lowest speed.

Add olive oil according to the preceeding "Cocktail Dip" recipe. When smooth and creamy, blend in the vinegar or lemon juice. Refrigerate at least an hour before serving.

Use as a dip for chips or raw vegetables.

MAKES 1 1/2 CUPS.

Curry especial

Special Curry Dip

2 tablespoons olive oil · 2 teaspoons curry powder · 1 tablespoon onion, minced · 1 tablespoon parsley, chopped · 1 teaspoon dried dill weed · 1/2 pint (1 cup) sour cream · 1 cup Spanish Mayonnaise (page 26) ·

In a small saucepan heat olive oil with curry powder over low heat for 3 minutes. Add the remaining ingredients. Chill 3 hours or overnight. Use as dip for raw vegetables, shrimp, chips, and crackers.

MAKES 2 CUPS.

Crema para aperitivos

Cocktail Dip

1 egg yolk · 1 garlic clove, crushed · 2 anchovy filets, chopped · 1/2 cup olive oil · 1/2 teaspoon lemon juice · 1 teaspoon Worcestershire sauce · 1 1/2 teaspoons mix of Italian salad dressing ·

Mix egg yolk, garlic, and anchovies in an electric mixer or blender at lowest speed.

Add olive oil drop by drop at first to avoid curdling. As the mixture begins to thicken, the oil may be added in a thin stream. When smooth and creamy, blend in the lemon juice, Worcestershire sauce, and Italian dressing mix. Refrigerate until cold.

Use as a dip for raw vegetables; such as carrots, cucumbers, cauliflower (separated into flowerets), or celery.

MAKES 3/4 CUP.

las salsas

3

sauces

Sauces are primarily served with fish. However, they may be an accompaniment for meat and vegetable dishes or salads. The most famous of all Spanish sauces is alioli, a mayonnaise-garlic sauce served with seafood, meat (such as steak and hamburgers), and vegetables (potatoes, artichokes, turnips, or carrots). In Spain the garlic is crushed in a mortar and the sauce is served in that mortar. However, a garlic press will produce the same results. Alioli was probably introduced to Spain by the Romans during the conquest, for the name itself is derived from the Latin.

Alioli

Ali-Oli Sauce

2 egg yolks ·
2 cloves garlic, crushed ·
1 teaspoon salt ·
1/2 teaspoon dry mustard (optional) ·
1 cup olive oil ·
1 tablespoon vinegar (or 1/2 tablespoon lemon juice) ·

Place room-temperature egg yolks, garlic, salt, and mustard (if you are adding it) in an electric mixer or blender. Mix at the lowest speed. Add olive oil drop by drop at first to avoid curdling. As the mixture begins to thicken, add the oil in a thin stream. When smooth and creamy, blend in the vinegar or lemon juice.

Refrigerate at least an hour before using. Will keep 3 or 4 days if refrigerated.

MAKES 1 1/2 CUPS OF SAUCE.

Mayonesa española

Spanish Mayonnaise

Ali-oli sauce without the garlic, this may be used in any recipe requiring mayonnaise as an ingredient; or, for a real treat for your guests, try this as a dip for chips. To prepare, see instructions on page 26.

Salsa mayonesa verde

Green Mayonnaise

**2 egg yolks ·
1 teaspoon salt ·
1 cup olive oil ·
1/2 tablespoon
lemon juice ·
1/2 cup minced
parsley · 1-2 drops
green food coloring
(optional) ·**

Place the room-temperature egg yolks and salt in an electric mixer or blender. Mix at lowest speed. Add olive oil drop by drop at first to prevent curdling. Continue to add all the oil in a thin stream until the mixture is smooth and creamy.

Blend in lemon juice, parsley, and food coloring for a green color.

Refrigerate at least an hour before serving. Serve over vegetables, chicken, or turkey.

MAKES 1 1/2 CUPS.

Salsa mayonesa de lima

Lime Mayonnaise

This is an excellent sauce with boiled shrimp.

2 egg yolks ·
1 teaspoon salt ·
1/2 teaspoon dry
mustard · 1 cup
olive oil ·
1/2 tablespoon
lemon juice ·
1/2 tablespoon
lime juice ·

Proceed as in the preceding recipe for "Green Mayonnaise" placing the egg yolks, salt, and mustard in a mixer or blender. Mix at low speed. Add the oil drop by drop at first; continue to add in a thin stream until all the oil is used and the mixture is smooth and creamy.

Blend in lemon and lime juice, and refrigerate at least one hour before serving.

This is an excellent sauce with boiled shrimp.

MAKES 1 1/2 CUPS.

Salsa mayonesa con tomate y coñac

Tomato and Cognac Mayonnaise

1 egg · juice of
1/2 lemon ·
1 teaspoon salt ·
1 cup olive oil ·
1 teaspoon
French's prepared
mustard ·
1 teaspoon tomato
paste ·
1 tablespoon
cognac ·

Mix the whole egg, one-half of the lemon juice, and the salt in an electric mixer or blender at low speed. Add oil according to the preceding recipe "Lime Mayonnaise."

Blend in the remaining lemon juice, mustard, tomato paste, and cognac. Refrigerate at least an hour before serving.

MAKES 1 1/2 CUPS.

Salsa para ensalada de fruta

Fruit Salad Dressing

2 egg yolks ·
1 teaspoon salt ·
1/2 tablespoon
lemon juice · 1 cup
olive oil · 1 cup
cottage cheese ·
1/2 tablespoon
lime juice · toasted
coconut or nuts ·

Mix the eggs, salt, and lemon juice in an electric mixer or blender at low speed. Add oil drop by drop at first. As the mixture thickens, the oil may be added in a thin stream. Continue to blend until smooth and creamy; then add the cottage cheese and lime juice; beat until smooth.

Refrigerate and serve over fresh or canned fruit. Sprinkle toasted coconut or nuts on each serving.

MAKES 2 1/2 CUPS OF SALAD DRESSING.

Salsa béchamel corriente

Basic Béchamel Sauce

Spaniards serve béchamel sauce as a side dish or use it as a basic ingredient in a recipe. There are many variations of this recipe that you may like to try, but for a medium sauce the flour should equal the butter and oil.

2 tablespoons
butter ·
2 tablespoons olive
oil · 4 tablespoons
flour · 1 teaspoon
salt · 2 cups cold
milk ·

In a heavy skillet over low heat, melt the butter with the oil; blend in the flour and salt. Remove from the heat and gradually stir in the milk. Return to the heat; stir constantly with a wooden spoon until the sauce is thick and smooth. If a thinner sauce is desired, add more cold milk.

MAKES 2 CUPS OF SAUCE.

Salsa béchamel con tomate

Béchamel Sauce with Tomato

Follow the preceding recipe for "Basic Béchamel Sauce" stirring until the sauce is smooth. Place a small amount of sauce in a cup and stir in two tablespoons of tomato paste. Add this to the sauce in the skillet and blend evenly.

MAKES 2 CUPS OF SAUCE.

Salsa béchamel con yemas

Béchamel Sauce with Egg Yolks

Follow the recipe for "Basic Béchamel Sauce" stirring until the sauce is smooth. Beat 3 egg yolks in a small bowl. Add one-half cup of the béchamel sauce to the yolks a very little at a time, stirring continually to keep the mixture from curdling. Add this to the sauce in the skillet, and stir to an even blend.

MAKES 2 CUPS OF SAUCE.

Salsa béchamel con alcaparras

Béchamel Sauce with Capers

Follow the recipe for "Basic Béchamel Sauce" stirring until the sauce is smooth. Beat 2 egg yolks in a small bowl. Add one-half cup of the béchamel sauce to the yolks a very little at a time, stirring continually to keep the mixture from curdling. Blend this with the sauce in the skillet. Just before serving, stir in 2 tablespoons of capers.

Serve with broiled or baked fish.

MAKES 2 CUPS OF SAUCE.

Salsa holandesa

Hollandaise Sauce

1/2 cup butter ·
3 egg yolks ·
1/4 teaspoon salt ·
1/2 cup hot water ·
juice of 1 lemon ·

Melt the butter in the top of a double boiler. Remove from the heat and add the egg yolks one at a time stirring continually with a wooden spoon.

Add the salt and slowly add the hot water stirring until the ingredients are blended.

Return to heat but keep the water in the bottom pan below the boiling stage. Stir continually for 7 to 10 minutes until the mixture is thick. Remove from the heat and stir in the lemon juice.

Serve immediately with vegetables, fish, or eggs.

MAKES 6 SERVINGS.

Salsa a la Granadina

Granada Sauce

1 medium tomato,
peeled and chopped ·
1 tablespoon
onion, chopped ·
1/3 teaspoon
ground cumin ·
1 teaspoon crushed
dried mint or
1 tablespoon
chopped fresh mint ·
1 tablespoon olive
oil · 1/4 cup sour
cream ·
1/4 teaspoon salt ·

Mix all of the ingredients together or purée in a blender.

Serve at room temperature as a sauce for meat or seafood.

MAKES 1 CUP.

Salsa blanca

Super-Smooth White Sauce

Use as a sauce for vegetables, or for a main dish, add any type of cooked meat and serve with rice.

3 tablespoons olive oil · 3 tablespoons flour · 1/4 teaspoon salt · 1/2 teaspoon dry mustard · 3/4 cup milk · 3/4 cup half-and-half or light cream ·

In a small saucepan, blend the flour in the oil; add the salt and mustard.

Over low heat gradually stir in the milk and cream. Stir continually until the mixture is thick and smooth.

MAKES 1 1/2 CUPS.

Salsa de queso

Cheese Sauce

Follow the preceding recipe for "Super-Smooth White Sauce" but add 1/3 cup of grated Cheddar, Mozzarella, Bleu, or Swiss cheese.

Salsa de tomate

Tomato Sauce

Follow the recipe for "Super-Smooth White Sauce" and add 1 1/2 tablespoons of tomato paste or 2 tablespoons of catsup.

Salsa verde

Green Sauce

Follow the recipe for "Super-Smooth White Sauce" and add 1/4 cup of finely chopped parsley or the tops of green onions. Serve with any type of fish.

Salsa condimentada

Seasoned Sauce

Follow the recipe for "Super-Smooth White Sauce" and add 3/4 teaspoon of either garlic or onion salt. Top with paprika. Serve with green beans or asparagus.

Salsa con crema cortada

Sour Cream Sauce

This sauce can be served as a side dish with pork, or as a topping for cauliflower or sliced tomatoes. Also, this is a good salad dressing.

1 tablespoon olive oil · 1 garlic clove, crushed · 1 tablespoon chives, chopped · 1 cup (8 oz.) sour cream ·

Heat the oil with the garlic and chives for several minutes over low heat. Remove from heat; stir in the sour cream. Refrigerate and serve cold.

MAKES 1 CUP OF SAUCE.

Crema cortada con eneldo

Sour Cream with Dill

A delicious sauce served with any type of cooked fish, as a dip for shrimp, or as a topping with sliced cucumbers.

1 tablespoon olive oil · 1 teaspoon dill seeds · 1 cup (8 oz.) sour cream ·

Heat the oil with the dill seeds over very low heat in order to bring out the flavor of the dill. Remove from heat; blend in the sour cream. Refrigerate before serving.

MAKES 1 CUP OF SAUCE.

Crema cortada con semillas de mostaza

Sour Cream with Mustard Seeds

Try this sauce served warm over cooked cabbage. Also, it is excellent with ham or corned beef.

1 tablespoon olive oil · 1 teaspoon mustard seeds · 1 cup (8 oz.) sour cream ·

Heat the oil with the mustard seeds over very low heat. Remove from heat; blend in the sour cream.

MAKES 1 CUP OF SAUCE.

Crema cortada con semillas de comino

Sour Cream with Cumin Seeds

This is an excellent sauce for a green vegetable, such as green beans, or served with chicken or turkey.

Follow the preceding recipe for "Sour Cream with Mustard Seeds" substituting a teaspoon of cumin seeds for the 1 teaspoon of mustard seeds.

MAKES 1 CUP OF SAUCE.

Crema cortada con polvo de "curry"

Sour Cream with Curry Powder

Notice that the word "curry" in Spanish is a foreign word originating in India; thus the same word is used in both Spanish and English.

Use this delicious spread for roast beef or ham sandwiches.

1 tablespoon olive oil · 1 teaspoon curry powder · 1 cup (8 oz.) sour cream · Heat the oil with the curry powder over very low fire. Remove from heat; blend in sour cream. Refrigerate before serving.

MAKES 1 CUP OF SPREAD.

Crema cortada con pellejos de limón

Sour Cream with Lemon Rind

May be served with asparagus as a substitute for Hollandaise Sauce or a very tasty complement for poached fish.

Follow the preceding recipe for "Sour Cream with Curry Powder" substituting 1 teaspoon of grated lemon rind for the curry powder.

MAKES 1 CUP OF SAUCE.

Salsa Romesco

Romesco Sauce

Romesco is a specialty of the provinces along the northern Mediterranean coast, like Tarragona and Barcelona. It is a potent sauce, or as the Spanish say, "una salsa fuerte." This sauce goes well with shell fish (lobster), cod fish, or vegetables.

39

2 small red chili peppers, dried · 1 medium tomato, peeled and seeded · 10 almonds, blanched and toasted · 3 cloves garlic, peeled · 1 teaspoon salt · 3/4 cup olive oil · 1/4 cup vinegar ·

Soak the pepper overnight in cold water.

Mix the tomato, almonds, garlic, salt, and peppers in an electric blender or food processor. The natives use a mortar and pestle to grind these.

Gradually add the olive oil. As the sauce thickens, slowly add the vinegar.

May be stored in the refrigerator for weeks.

MAKES 1 1/2 CUPS OF SAUCE.

Salsa de perejil

Parsley Sauce

1 cup fresh parsley sprigs · 1 clove garlic · 1/4 cup olive oil · 2 tablespoons wine vinegar · salt and pepper, to taste ·

Mix parsley, garlic, and oil in an electric blender or food processor until smooth.

Blend in vinegar, salt, and pepper.

Serve over fish.

MAKES 4 TO 6 SERVINGS.

Salsa de ajo

Garlic Sauce

This is a good sauce for hamburgers, veal or pork chops, and vegetables.

1 cup olive oil · 1 medium potato, boiled and mashed · 2 cloves garlic, minced · 2 tablespoons wine vinegar · 1/2 teaspoon salt · pepper, few grains ·

Gradually add the olive oil to the potato and garlic. You may use an electric mixer. Stir in the vinegar, salt, and pepper.

MAKES 1 1/2 CUPS OF SAUCE.

Salsa de almendras y pimientos

Almond and Hot Pepper Sauce

Any type of meat or seafood may be served with this sauce.

1 egg · 1/4 cup almonds, blanched and toasted · 1 small ripe tomato, peeled and seeded · 1 clove garlic, minced · 1/4 cup wine vinegar · 1 teaspoon salt · 1/4 teaspoon cayenne pepper · 1 cup olive oil ·

Blend the egg, almonds, tomato, garlic, vinegar, salt, pepper, and one-fourth cup of the olive oil in an electric blender or food processor until smooth. Add the remaining oil slowly, continuing to blend at high speed until the mixture thickens.

MAKES 1 1/2 CUPS OF SAUCE.

Salsa a la italiana

Italian-style Sauce

This sauce may be served with spaghetti, fried eggplant, meat, or fish.

1/4 cup olive oil · 1 cup onion, chopped · 1 clove garlic · 1/2 cup fresh parsley, minced · 3/4 cup tomato paste · 2 1/2 cups canned tomatoes · 1 teaspoon sugar · 1/4 teaspoon salt · 1/8 teaspoon pepper ·

Heat the onion and garlic in the oil until tender—about 3 minutes. Mash the garlic; add parsley, tomato paste, tomatoes with liquid, sugar, salt, and pepper. When the mixture boils, lower the heat to simmer. Cook 1 hour, stirring occasionally.

MAKES 5 CUPS OF SAUCE.

las sopas

4

soups

Soup is a very important and necessary element of the Spanish meal. It normally constitutes the first course in the main meal of the day served around two o'clock in the afternoon, but may well be the only course for a light evening supper. As the Iberian Peninsula is surrounded by water on three sides, soup made from varieties of fish is very popular, and each region has its own fish soup specialty.

The one soup originating in Spain that has gained overnight popularity in the United States is GAZPACHO, sometimes called the "salad soup." It was created in southern Spain in the province of Andalusia. As this area is extremely hot, one can understand the popularity of a soup served icy cold. There are numerous restaurants in northern Spain today where gazpacho is not served and was relatively unknown until a few years ago. However, the popularity of this southern soup has spread to most of the other provinces of the peninsula, where each had added its own flair to the original recipe.

Canned gazpacho is available in many supermarkets in the United States; but, if you are having guests, by all means make your own. You may serve gazpacho as the first course of a formal meal; or for a real treat, serve it in cups as an appetizer for party fare.

Gazpacho básico

Basic Gazpacho

2 slices white bread, crusts removed and cut in cubes · 2 cloves garlic, crushed · 1/4 cup olive oil · 1/2 cup water · 1 teaspoon salt · 2 pounds ripe tomatoes, peeled and chopped (or substitute 3 cups good quality canned tomatoes with liquid) · 1/4 small cucumber, chopped · 1/4 cup onions, grated · 2 tablespoons wine vinegar · 2 cups ice water ·

Combine bread, garlic, olive oil, water, and salt. Let stand overnight.

In an electric blender, mixer, or food processor, add the tomatoes and cucumber to the bread mixture; purée. Add the onions and refrigerate.

When ready to serve, blend in vinegar and ice water. If necessary, add more salt.

Serve with garnishes.

SERVES 8-10.

Garnishes

The garnishes are a MUST with gazpacho. Although these may be added to the soup by the cook, it is much more interesting to let each person add his or her own garnish served from individual bowls. Nearly any of the ingredients used in the soup may be used for garnish. It is not necessary to serve all of these listed, but be sure to try at least two of them.

CROUTONS Serve commercial croutons or fry small cubes of white bread in olive oil until golden brown.

TOMATOES Peel and slice fresh tomatoes in bite-size pieces.

CUCUMBERS Peel and slice a cucumber in small pieces.

ONIONS Peel and chop a small onion.

GREEN PEPPER Remove seeds; chop a small green bell pepper.

EGGS Hard cook 2 or 3 eggs for 12 minutes in water that is simmering but not boiling. Remove shells. Refrigerate until thoroughly chilled. Chop fine before serving.

ICE CUBES Serve plain, or freeze tomato juice in an ice cube tray and serve as an interesting and unusual complement to your gazpacho.

Gazpachuelo frío

Cold Gazpachuelo

3 egg yolks (or 2 whole eggs) ·
1 teaspoon salt ·
pepper, few grains ·
1 1/2 cups olive oil ·
1/2 cup red wine ·
3 1/2 cups ice water ·
2 large tomatoes, peeled and chopped ·
12-14 black olives, pitted ·

Prepare a mayonnaise by putting the room-temperature egg yolks or whole eggs, and the salt and pepper in an electric blender or food processor. Add the olive oil very slowly to avoid curdling. Blend until the mixture is smooth. Put in a soup tureen or large serving bowl.

Slowly stir in the wine and cold water. Garnish with tomatoes and olives. Serve cold.

SERVES 4-5.

Gazpachuelo caliente de pescado

Hot Gazpachuelo of Fish

This soup is prepared with any type of cleaned whole white fish, with both the head and the tail on. You may prefer to filet the fish in six serving pieces.

6 cups water ·
1 tablespoon salt ·
1 bay leaf ·
1/2 small onion,
quartered ·
2 tablespoons
white wine ·
1 1/2 pounds fish ·
6 small potatoes,
peeled and cut in
half · 2 eggs ·
1 1/2 tablespoons
vinegar or lemon
juice · salt and
pepper, to taste ·
1/3 cup olive oil ·

Bring the water to a boil with the salt, bay leaf, onion, wine, fish, and potatoes in a covered pot. Remove the potatoes when they are thoroughly cooked—after about 30 minutes. Strain the soup and return the broth to very low heat.

Prepare a mayonnaise by placing the room-temperature eggs, vinegar (or lemon juice), salt, and pepper in an electric blender. Slowly add the olive oil; blend until the mixture is smooth. Place in a soup tureen or large serving bowl.

Slowly add the broth to the mayonnaise. You may have to allow the broth to cool a little to avoid curdling the mayonnaise. Dice the potatoes, debone the fish, and serve warm.

SERVES 6.

Sopa de ajo sencillo

Simple Garlic Soup

6 slices day-old
bread, cubed ·
4 cloves of garlic ·
4 tablespoons olive
oil · 1 teaspoon
paprika · 6 cups
water · 4 chicken
bouillon cubes ·
salt, to taste ·

Sauté the bread and whole garlic cloves in hot olive oil until golden brown. Discard the garlic; mash the bread to a paste.

In the pot with the crushed bread, add the paprika, water, and bouillon cubes. Bring to a boil; lower the heat and simmer 10 minutes. Salt to taste and serve hot.

SERVES 6.

Sopa de ajo con huevos

Garlic Soup with Eggs

Each area of Spain seems to have a slightly different way of preparing "Sopa de ajo con huevos," but here is a favorite in Madrid.

4 slices day-old bread, cubed · 4 cloves garlic · 1/2 small onion, chopped · 1/4 cup olive oil · 1 teaspoon paprika · 5 cups water · 1 beef bouillon cube · 3 tomatoes, peeled and chopped · salt and pepper, to taste · 2 eggs, beaten ·

Brown the bread, garlic, and onion in hot oil. Remove the pan from the heat; stir in the paprika using a wooden spoon. Discard the garlic cloves.

Return the pan to the heat. Add the water, bouillon, and tomatoes; salt and pepper to taste. Bring to a boil; then, reduce the heat, cover the pan, and simmer about 20 minutes.

Mix the beaten eggs with about 1 cup of the hot broth. Beat to blend and return to the pan; simmer for 1 minute. Do not allow the soup to boil. Serve immediately.

SERVES 6.

Sopa de cebolla

Onion Soup

3 tablespoons olive oil · 2 medium onions, sliced · 2 tablespoons flour · 6 cups canned beef broth (or substitute 6 cups water with 6 bouillon cubes) · salt and pepper, to taste · 1 tablespoon parsley, finely chopped · Parmesan cheese, grated ·

Heat the oil; add onions and simmer about 10 minutes or until they begin to brown. Remove onions. Add flour and stir for several minutes until it begins to brown. Slowly add broth stirring with a wooden spoon. Return the onions to the pan; bring to a boil; lower heat and simmer 20 minutes. Salt and pepper to taste.

Put in a soup tureen or serve from individual bowls. Garnish with parsley and cheese, or pass the cheese separately.

SERVES 6.

48

Sopa de jugo de tomate

Tomato Juice Soup

2 cups canned beef bouillon, or 2 cups water with 2 bouillon cubes · 1 tablespoon corn starch · 2 cups tomato juice · 2 tablespoons dry sherry · salt and pepper, to taste · 1/3 cup whipping cream, whipped · parsley, chopped ·

Dilute the corn starch in 1 cup of the bouillon. Combine this with the remaining bouillon, tomato juice, sherry, salt and pepper. Cook for 10 minutes.

Top each serving with whipped cream and a sprinkle of parsley.

NOTE: This soup may be served cold by eliminating the corn starch and refrigerating the soup before serving.

SERVES 4.

Sopa de tomate y judías verdes

Tomato and Green Bean Soup

6 cups cold water · 1/2 pound potatoes, peeled and cut in half · 3 pounds very ripe tomatoes · 2 tablespoons bacon grease · 1 parsley sprig · 1 bay leaf · salt, to taste · 1/2 pound green string beans · 1/8 teaspoon bicarbonate of soda

To the cold water, add the potatoes, tomatoes, bacon grease, parsley, bay leaf, and salt. Bring to a boil and cook for 45 minutes or until the potatoes are soft. Allow to cool slightly; remove parsley and bay leaf; mash potatoes and tomatoes together. Put in a soup tureen.

While the tomato mixture is cooking, snap the green beans in 2-inch pieces. Cook in boiling water to which soda has been added so the beans will retain their color. Cook 30 minutes or until tender. Add the green beans to the soup tureen. Do not stir, for the beans should remain on top. Serve warm.

SERVES 6.

Sopa de cebollas y patatas

Onion and Potato Soup

2 medium onions,
diced ·
3 tablespoons olive
oil · 6 cups water ·
4 beef bouillon
cubes · 6 medium
potatoes, peeled
and sliced in small
pieces · salt ·

Brown the onions lightly in the oil. Add the water, bouillon cubes, and potatoes. Add the salt, but sparingly as the bouillon cubes are salty.

Bring to a rapid boil; lower the heat and cook about 30 minutes or until the potatoes are very tender. Serve hot.

SERVES 6.

Crema de esparragos

Cream of Asparagus

4 tablespoons
butter ·
4 tablespoons flour ·
1 1/2 teaspoons
salt · pepper, few
grains · 2 cups
milk · 2 pounds
asparagus · 6 cups
water · 4 cups
asparagus liquid ·
2 egg yolks ·
1 sprig parsley,
chopped ·

Melt the butter; mix in the flour, salt, and pepper with a wooden spoon. Remove from heat; gradually blend in the milk. Return to low heat and continue to stir until the mixture is smooth.

In a separate pan, cook the asparagus, cut in lengths of 1 1/2 inches, in 6 cups of boiling water to which salt has been added. When the asparagus is tender, put the tips aside, and blend the rest in an electric blender or food processor. Reserve 4 cups of the liquid in which the asparagus cooked.

Add the blended asparagus to the milk mixture. Slowly add the reserved asparagus liquid stirring continually.

Remove a little of the soup to cool. Add the egg yolks to this cooler mixture so they won't curdle.

Blend this mixture in a soup tureen or large serving bowl with the hot soup. Add the asparagus tips; garnish with parsley.

SERVES 6.

Crema de berros

Cream of Watercress

3 tablespoons olive oil · 1 medium onion, sliced · 6 medium potatoes, sliced · 2 bunches watercress, cleaned and chopped · 6 cups hot water, salted · 2 beef bouillon cubes · 1 cup milk · salt and pepper, to taste ·

Heat the oil; add onion and simmer 5 to 10 minutes, stirring with a wooden spoon. Add potatoes and 1 3/4 bunches of the watercress. Put the other 1/4 aside for garnish. Add the water to which a little salt has been added and the bouillon cubes. Simmer covered for an hour. Add milk, salt (if necessary) and pepper; cook over very low heat for 15 minutes.

Serve from a soup tureen or individual bowls garnished with fresh watercress.

SERVES 6.

Crema de espinacas

Cream of Spinach

1 pound spinach · 1/2 cup water · 1/2 teaspoon salt · 2 tablespoons butter · 2 tablespoons oil · 1/2 medium onion, chopped · 4 tablespoons flour · 1 1/2 teaspoons salt · pepper, few grains · 2 cups milk · 1 egg yolk, beaten · 2 1/2 cups spinach pulp and liquid · croutons (optional) ·

Select spinach leaves that are dark green in color. Wash thoroughly under running water. Discard roots and stems.

Cook in heavy pan with water and salt over low heat. When more liquid accumulates in the pan from the spinach leaves, increase heat to medium, cover and cook 10 minutes. Stir once or twice during cooking time. Press through sieve. Reserve liquid.

While the spinach is cooking prepare a béchamel sauce by melting the butter with the oil over low heat. Simmer the onion until soft, about 5 minutes. Blend in the flour, salt, and pepper.

Remove from the heat and gradually blend in the milk. Return to low heat and stir continually until thick and smooth.

51

Put the egg yolk in a cup; mix a little of the béchamel with the egg and return to heat.

Measure 2 1/2 cups of the spinach pulp and the liquid in which the spinach was cooked. Add water if necessary.

Mix the spinach mixture and béchamel together in a soup tureen or large serving bowl. Serve warm with croutons, if desired.

SERVES 6.

Crema de champiñones

Cream of Mushroom

1/4 pound fresh mushrooms, washed and chopped · 1/4 cup butter · 2 tablespoons onion, finely chopped · 1 teaspoon lemon juice · 1 teaspoon salt · 4 tablespoons flour · 4 cups canned beef broth · 2 cups milk · 1 egg yolk, beaten ·

Simmer the mushrooms in the butter with the onion, lemon juice, and salt until the mushrooms are soft—about 15 minutes.

Put the flour in another pan; stir with a wooden spoon until the flour begins to take on color—about 10 minutes. Slowly add the cold broth to the flour. Stir continually for about 10 minutes until the mixture is smooth. Add the mushrooms and milk; cook on very low heat for 5 more minutes.

Put the egg yolk in a soup tureen or large serving bowl. Add the soup slowly, stirring with a wooden spoon. Serve hot.

SERVES 6.

Crema de apio

Cream of Celery

3 tablespoons butter · 2 medium onions, diced · 3 tablespoons flour · 1 1/2 teaspoons salt · pepper, few grains · 2 cups milk · 2 1/2 cups celery, finely chopped · 4 cups water · 2 beef bouillon cubes · 2 egg yolks, beaten · 1/2 cup cream · parsley ·

Make a sauce by melting the butter over low heat and simmering the onions until they are soft. Blend in the flour, salt, and pepper. Remove from heat and slowly add milk. Stir continually over low heat until smooth.

In a separate pan, cook the celery in water with the bouillon cubes over low heat until the celery is tender. Pour this slowly in the sauce mixture. Add more salt if necessary.

Put the egg yolks and cream in a soup tureen or large serving bowl. Add the soup very slowly to keep the eggs and cream from curdling. Garnish with parsley and serve immediately.

SERVES 6.

Caldo gallego

Galician-style Broth

1/2 cup dried white beans · 1 ham bone with some meat · 1/4 pound salt pork · 1/2 pound beef, sliced in large pieces · 8 cups water · 2 medium potatoes, peeled and chopped · 1/2 small head cabbage, sliced · 3 turnips, quartered, and tops, chopped · salt and pepper, to taste ·

Soak the beans in water for three hours before cooking. Then put the drained beans, ham, salt pork, and beef in a pot with 8 cups of cold water. Bring to a boil; reduce heat and simmer covered for 2 1/2 hours.

Add the potatoes, cabbage, the turnips cut in fourths, the turnip greens, cleaned and chopped, and salt and pepper to taste. Simmer for 1 hour and serve hot.

NOTE: This broth is better if it is prepared the day before it is to be served and reheated.

SERVES 6-8.

Pote gallego

Galician-style Pot

This is very much like Galician broth but is thicker and may be served as a main course.

1 cup dried white beans · 1/2 pound smoked ham · 1 beef meat bone · 1/2 pound beef, sliced in large pieces · 1/4 pound salt pork · 8 cups water · 1/2 medium head of cabbage, sliced · 4 turnips, quartered · turnip greens, chopped · 4 medium potatoes, peeled and chopped ·

Follow the instructions in the previous recipe for "Galician-style Broth."

SERVES 6-8.

Caldo de habas

Lima Bean Broth

1 1/2 cups dried lima beans · 10 cups water · 1 cup cooked ham, diced · 1 large onion, chopped · 1 garlic clove, crushed · add salt and pepper, to taste · 1/2 pound chorizo or pepperoni sausage · 2 medium potatoes, chopped · 1 medium turnip, chopped ·

Soak the beans overnight in cold water. Drain. Put 10 cups of water in a large pan with the beans. Bring to a rapid boil; cover and remove from the heat. Set aside for 1 to 1 1/2 hours.

Add ham, onion, garlic, salt, and pepper to the beans. Bring to a rapid boil. Reduce the heat and simmer 1 hour.

Prick the sausage in several places with a needle or fork so it will not burst. Add the sausage, potatoes, and turnip to the soup. Simmer 30 more minutes.

Remove the sausage and cut in bite-size pieces.

Put the sausage and the soup in a tureen or large serving bowl and serve hot.

SERVES 6-8.

Caldo de cocido con arroz

Broth Cooked with Rice

8 cups of canned beef or chicken broth ·
8 tablespoons rice ·
2 hard-boiled eggs ·
1 tablespoon parsley, chopped ·

Bring the broth to a boil; add rice. When it boils again, lower heat and cook slowly for 15 minutes, more or less. Read the instructions on the package, for the cooking time for rice varies.

Shell and chop the hard-boiled eggs.

Pour the soup in a tureen or large bowl and garnish with parsley and chopped eggs. Serve immediately.

SERVES 6.

Caldo al minuto

Minute Broth

1 pound round steak, sliced ·
1 beef soup bone ·
6 cups water ·
1 small onion, chopped ·
2 medium carrots, peeled and sliced ·
1 sprig parsley ·
1 garlic clove, crushed · 1/3 bay leaf · 1 1/2 tablespoons olive oil ·
1 1/2 tablespoons of white wine ·
3/4 teaspoon salt ·

Put meat and bone in the water. Bring to a boil. Reduce heat; cover, and simmer 2 hours.

Add onion, carrots, parsley, garlic, bay leaf, oil, wine, and salt. Bring to a boil again; lower heat to medium and cook 30 minutes.

Remove foam and serve with the vegetables, or pass through a sieve reserving the liquid for recipes requiring beef broth.

MAKES ABOUT 3 CUPS OF BROTH.

Crema de gallina

Cream of Chicken

6 cups canned chicken broth · 1 garlic clove · 1 tablespoon parsley, chopped · 1/2 bay leaf · 1 teaspoon salt · pepper, few grains · 2 breasts of chicken · 1/2 cup celery, chopped with leaves · 2 medium carrots, cut in large pieces · 1 medium onion, chopped · 1 tablespoon butter · 1 tablespoon olive oil · 2 tablespoons flour · 1 cup milk · 1 egg yolk (optional) ·

Bring chicken broth to a boil; add garlic, parsley, bay leaf, salt, pepper, chicken breasts, celery, carrots, and onion. Lower the heat; simmer about 1 1/2 hours or until the chicken is tender.

Remove chicken from the broth. Debone; cut in bite-size pieces and set aside.

Heat the butter and oil in a skillet; blend in the flour. Remove from heat and gradually add the milk. Be very careful that the mixture does not become lumpy; continue to stir until well blended.

If you are adding the egg yolk, mix it lightly with a cup of broth that has cooled slightly; then add it to the soup.

Return the chicken to the broth. Stir in the milk mixture. Remove garlic clove and bay leaf. Serve immediately.

SERVES 6.

Sopa de fideos simples

Simple Vermicelli Soup

2 quarts (8 cups) of broth · 4 ounces of vermicelli · salt, to taste ·

You may use canned beef or chicken broth or powder or cubes to make the broth. To prepare your own beef broth, follow the instructions for "Minute Broth," (page 55).

Bring the broth to a boil. Add the vermicelli a little at a time; lower the heat and cook slowly for 15 minutes, or follow the cooking instructions on the package. Do not overcook. Add salt to taste. Serve immediately as this soup should not be reheated.

SERVES 6.

Sopa de verduras

Vegetable Soup

2 quarts cold water ·
1 beef soup bone ·
3 teaspoons salt ·
1/4 teaspoon
pepper ·
1 tablespoon olive
oil · 1 cup carrots,
sliced · 1/2 cup
turnips, diced ·
2 medium onions,
sliced · 3 large
potatoes, diced ·
1 stalk of celery,
sliced ·
1 tablespoon corn
starch ·

Bring the water with the bone, salt, pepper, and oil to a boil. Lower the heat and simmer 30 minutes.

Add carrots, turnips, onions, potatoes, and celery. Bring to a boil again. Lower the heat and simmer 30 minutes more, or until the vegetables are tender.

Dissolve the corn starch in a little cold water. Stir in a little broth from the soup. Add this to the soup stirring with a wooden spoon. Cook for 5 minutes. Remove bone and serve from a tureen or large serving bowl.

SERVES 6.

Sopa de apio y patatas

Celery and Potato Soup

3 tablespoons olive
oil · 3 stalks celery,
cleaned and
chopped ·
2 medium onions,
chopped ·
2 1/2 cups
potatoes, peeled
and diced · 8 cups
water ·
1 1/2 teaspoons
salt · green celery
leaves, chopped or
chopped parsley ·

Simmer the celery and onions in the oil about 10 minutes or until they begin to color. Add potatoes, water, and salt. Bring to a boil; lower the heat and simmer 1 hour. Serve very hot, topping each serving with celery leaves or parsley for garnish.

SERVES 6-8.

Potaje de garbanzos

Chickpea Thick Soup

1/2 pound chickpeas · 10 cups water · 6 ounces codfish or white fish filets · 2 medium ripe tomatoes, peeled and chopped · 2 1/2 garlic cloves · 1 bay leaf · 1/2 pound spinach · 1 sprig parsley · 3 tablespoons oil · 1 large onion, chopped · 1 tablespoon flour · 1 teaspoon paprika · salt, to taste ·

Soak the chickpeas overnight in enough water to cover to which a little salt has been added.

The following day put 10 cups of lukewarm water in a large pot. Add the drained chickpeas, the uncooked fish cut in large pieces, the tomatoes, 2 of the whole garlic cloves, and the bay leaf. Bring to a boil; lower the heat and simmer 2 hours.

Clean the spinach by discarding the stems and wash under running water for several minutes. Chop. After the chickpeas have cooked 2 hours, add the spinach and cook together another 30 minutes.

Crush the remaining 1/2 clove of garlic with the sprig of parsley in a mortar and pestle or food processor.

Heat the oil in a frying pan; add the onions. Stir with a wooden spoon until the onions become transparent (about 5 minutes). Add flour, crushed garlic, parsley, and paprika. Cook another 5 minutes being careful not to burn the paprika. Stir this mixture into the soup pot; add salt to taste. Simmer another 15 minutes. Remove the 2 whole garlic cloves and the bay leaf before serving. Serve hot.

You may wish to serve this soup with fish balls.

2 small pieces of white fish filets, uncooked · 1 garlic clove, crushed · 1 tablespoon onion, minced · 1 egg · 2 tablespoons bread crumbs · 1/2 cup flour ·

Mix all of the ingredients thoroughly (except flour) in an electric blender or food processor. Form balls about 1-inch in diameter. Cover with flour.

Bring the soup to a boil; add fish balls and cook about 5 minutes. Serve the fish balls in the soup.

SERVES 6-8.

Puré de garbanzos

Chickpea Purée

2 tablespoons olive oil · 2 medium onions, chopped · 6 cups canned beef or chicken broth · 1 tablespoon corn meal · 1 pound of chickpeas, cooked · 1 teaspoon salt · squares of bread, fried ·

Lightly brown the onions in oil. Add 1 cup of broth; simmer for 5 minutes.

Dissolve the corn meal in 2 tablespoons of the cold broth.

In a large pot, heat the remaining broth and onion mixture.

Purée the chickpeas in a blender, mixer or food processor. (Directions for cooking the chickpeas should be on the package, or you can follow the recipe for "Chickpea Thick Soup" on page 58.)

Add the chickpeas, corn meal, and salt to the broth. Bring to a boil; boil slowly for 5 minutes.

Serve with croutons or little squares of bread fried to a golden brown in oil.

SERVES 6.

Sopa de repollo

Cabbage Soup

1 pound head of cabbage · 3 tablespoons olive oil · 3 strips of bacon, cut in small pieces · 1 large onion, chopped · 8 cups water, boiled · 4 beef bouillon cubes · 4 tablespoons rice · 1 teaspoon salt ·

Wash the cabbage; drain well, and cut in fine strips. If you have a food processor, use the cutting blade for 10 seconds or less.

Heat the bacon in the oil; fry the onion until it begins to brown. Add the cabbage; cover the pot, but stir from time to time with a wooden spoon. After 15 minutes, add the boiling water, bouillon cubes, rice, and salt. Simmer 1 hour. Serve hot.

SERVES 6.

Sopa marinera

Seaman's Soup

3 tablespoons olive oil · 2 medium scallions, chopped · 1/4 cup onions, chopped · 2 medium tomatoes, peeled and sliced · 1/2 bay leaf · 2 garlic cloves, crushed · 1 pound shrimp · 1/2 pound white fish · 8 cups water · 2 teaspoons salt · 1/2 teaspoon saffron · 3/4 cup (6 oz.) noodles · 1/4 teaspoon pepper ·

Sauté the scallions and onions in the oil slowly for 5 minutes. Add tomatoes, bay leaf, garlic, shrimp (cleaned but in their shells), fish, water, and salt. Bring to a boil, and boil for 15 to 20 minutes. Remove the shrimp and fish. Strain the broth through a sieve.

Debone the fish, shell shrimp. Chop together with the saffron and a little of the broth. Return this fish mixture to the broth. Add noodles, pepper and more salt, if necessary. Cook over medium heat for 15 to 20 minutes, or until the noodles are tender.

Serve in a tureen or large bowl.

SERVES 6.

Crema de gambas o cangrejos

Cream of Shrimp or Crab

FOR THE BROTH: 8 cups water · 1 cup dry white wine · 2 medium carrots, diced · 1 medium onion, sliced in four pieces · 1 parsley sprig · 1 small bay leaf · 2 teaspoons salt ·

Prepare the broth by combining the 7 ingredients in a pan. Bring to a boil. Simmer for 30 minutes; remove from heat and allow to cool completely. You may prepare the broth several hours ahead of time to allow for cooling.

Add the shrimp or crab meat to the cold broth. You may want to use both. Simmer 5 minutes on low heat. Remove the shrimp or crab meat from broth and mash with the butter to a purée. Bake this purée in the oven at 325° for 25 minutes.

Measure the broth to be sure you have six cups. If not, add water. Add the rice and cognac, additional

FOR THE SHRIMP OR CRAB MEAT:
1 pound shrimp, cleaned and shelled and/or 1 pound (6- or 8-oz. can) crab meat · 1/2 cup butter · 1/3 cup rice · 2 tablespoons cognac · salt and pepper, to taste ·

salt, if necessary, and a few grains of black pepper. Cook over slow heat for 15 minutes. Before serving, add the shrimp or crab meat. Cook an additional ten minutes, stirring from time to time with a wooden spoon. Remove bay leaf and serve warm.

SERVES 6-8.

Crema de gambas

Cream of Shrimp

1 pound fresh or frozen shrimp · 2 ounces butter · 2 tablespoons flour · 2 tablespoons tomato paste · 2 quarts chicken broth · 2 tablespoons cognac · salt and pepper, to taste · 1/2 cup heavy cream ·

If you are using frozen shrimp, follow the cooking directions on the package. For fresh shrimp, bring a quart of water (to which salt has been added) to a boil. Add shrimp; bring to a second boil; remove from heat and let stand 6 to 8 minutes. Allow to cool; remove shells.

Slice several of the shrimp and save for garnish. Pound the remaining shrimp with half of the butter.

Melt the remaining butter in a large pan. Gradually stir in the flour until it begins to brown. Add shrimp, tomato paste, and chicken broth. If you do not have any chicken broth on hand, you may use canned broth, or add 4 chicken bouillon cubes to the water. Cook over low heat for 30 minutes.

Pass through a sieve. Add cognac, salt, and pepper. Return to low heat for 5 minutes.

Put the cream in a soup tureen or large serving bowl. Add the soup slowly so the cream will not curdle.

Garnish with the sliced shrimp and serve hot.

SERVES 6.

Sopa de cuarto de hora

Quarter-of-an-Hour Soup

No Spanish cookbook is complete without including "Quarter-of-an-Hour Soup," although the name is misleading, for it cannot be prepared in fifteen minutes. This fresh fish soup is very popular, especially in Madrid. Even though this capital city is located in the center of the Peninsula, fresh fish is readily available from coastal regions.

2 tablespoons olive oil · 1/2 cup ham, diced · 1 medium onion, chopped fine · 2 small tomatoes, peeled and chopped · 5 cups hot water · 1/2 pound shrimp, cooked, shelled and chopped · 1 cup canned clams and liquid · 1/2 cup uncooked rice · 1/4 cup green peas, fresh or frozen · 1/2 teaspoon paprika · 1/2 teaspoon salt · black pepper, few grains · 2 hard-boiled eggs, chopped fine ·

Brown the ham in the olive oil and set aside. Sauté the onion in the oil until golden. Add the tomatoes to the onions; cook about 5 minutes or until the tomatoes are soft.

Add water, ham, cooked shrimp (prepared by following the instructions in the previous recipe for "Cream of Shrimp" soup), clams, and liquid. Bring to a boil; add rice, green peas, paprika, salt, and pepper. Boil 15 minutes. (Now you can see where the quarter-of-an-hour originated.)

Serve hot, garnishing each serving with chopped egg.

SERVES 6.

Sopa de mero

Fish Soup

3 tablespoons olive oil · 3/4 cup scallions, chopped · 1 cup onions, chopped · 4 cups water · 1 cup white wine · 1 pound white fish, cleaned and sliced · 1 fish head · 1 sprig parsley · 1 garlic clove · 1 bay leaf · 2 pounds potatoes, peeled and sliced in large pieces · salt, to taste · 1 cup milk · 2 egg yolks, beaten · parsley for garnish, chopped ·

Fry the scallions and onions in the oil until they begin to take on color. Add the water and wine. Bring to a boil, and add the fish, fish head, parsley, garlic, and bay leaf. Bring to a boil again; then add the potatoes and salt. Simmer 1 hour.

Remove and discard the fish head, garlic, and bay leaf. Remove the potatoes and fish from the broth. Debone the fish, and remove the skin. Mash the fish and potatoes with 1 cup of warm milk; return them to the broth. Slowly add some of the soup broth to the egg yolks; add this to the soup. Do not allow the soup to boil.

Serve hot, garnishing each serving with parsley.

SERVES 6-8.

los huevos

5

egg dishes

For those of us living near Mexico, the term tortilla can only mean a type of corn pancake, or more recently one made with flour. However, a tortilla in Spain is an omelet, which may be served as a separate course or together with a first course. In the United States, these omelets would be ideal for a light meal. They are delicious as are all the egg dishes of Spain.

HINTS FOR THE PREPARATION OF OMELETS   Allow 1 1/2 to 2 medium eggs per serving, and do not attempt to prepare an omelet with more than 4 large eggs at a time. The Spanish omelet generally is served flat; so a cast-iron skillet is ideal for the preparation. Although vegetable oil, butter, or other fat may be used, the Spanish will use olive oil, for it does not stick to the pan. Be sure to use sufficient oil to cover the bottom of the skillet.

If the recipe calls for a filling, prepare it first. Allow this mixture to cool 5 to 10 minutes before adding the eggs.

Tortilla a la española

Spanish-style Omelet

FOR THE FILLING:
2 tablespoons olive oil · 2 tablespoons green pepper, chopped · 2 tablespoons onion, chopped · 1 large tomato, peeled and chopped fine · 3 tablespoons celery, chopped fine · 1/4 cup mushrooms, sliced · 1/2 teaspoon salt · 1/4 teaspoon black pepper · 1/4 teaspoon cayenne pepper ·

FOR THE OMELET:
4 large eggs, separated · 1/2 teaspoon salt · black and cayenne pepper, few grains · 5 tablespoons hot water · 1 tablespoon olive oil ·

Heat the oil in a heavy skillet. Sauté the green pepper and onion until soft. Add tomato, celery, mushrooms, salt, pepper, and cayenne. Cook over low heat until the tomato is tender. Prepare the egg mixture while the filling is cooking.

Beat the egg yolks until thick and lemon-colored. Add salt, pepper, and hot water. Beat the egg whites until stiff but not dry. Fold the egg yolk mixture into the egg whites.

Heat the oil in a skillet. Pour in the egg mixture, spreading it evenly over the pan. Cook over low heat until the omelet begins to brown on the bottom. Finish cooking in a 350° oven for about 10 minutes. The top should be dry.

The omelet may be served flat with the tomato sauce as a side dish, or you may prefer to put half of the sauce on a serving plate and pour on remaining sauce. Serve at once.

SERVES 4.

Tortilla de patatas a la española

Spanish-style Potato Omelet

This is the most popular omelet served in Spain today.

3 medium-sized potatoes · 1 cup olive oil · salt, to taste · 4 large eggs · mayonnaise ·

Peel and wash the potatoes. Dry them on paper towels. Cut in two lengthwise; then slice very thin. A food processor may be used for this.

Heat the oil in a frying pan. Fry the potatoes slowly until lightly brown. Drain on paper towels; add salt to taste. Remove excess oil from the frying pan.

Beat the eggs with some additional salt—about 1/4 teaspoon. Stir in the potatoes. Measure 3 table-spoons of olive oil to cover the bottom of the frying pan. When hot, pour in the mixture of eggs and potatoes. Shake the frying pan occasionally to keep the omelet from sticking.

When one side is brown, cover the pan with a plate to turn the omelet, brown the other side.

Serve hot or cold accompanied with mayonnaise served in a separate dish.

SERVES 3-4.

Tortilla de patatas

Potato Omelet

This is a slightly different version of the preceding recipe.

3 medium-sized potatoes · 1 large onion, chopped · 1/2 garlic clove, crushed · 1/2 cup olive oil · salt · 4 large eggs ·

Prepare the potatoes as for "Spanish-style Potato Omelet." Fry them in the oil with the onion and garlic until the potatoes are lightly brown.

Beat the eggs and continue as in the preceding recipe.

SERVES 3-4.

Tortilla de jamón

Ham Omelet

1/2 cup ham, cubed · 3 tablespoons olive oil · 4 large eggs, beaten · salt, pinch ·

Fry the ham in the oil. Add the beaten eggs to which a little salt has been added, for the ham may be quite salty.

Shake the pan occasionally to keep the omelet from sticking. Continue to cook over low heat for several minutes until it is firm on the bottom. Cover the pan with a plate to turn the omelet; brown the other side and serve hot.

The omelet may be folded over, which is a French-style omelet, or served flat, Spanish-style.

SERVES 4.

Tortilla de atún

Tuna Omelet

5 tablespoons olive oil · 1 small onion, peeled and chopped · 1/2 cup canned tuna · 4 eggs, beaten · salt, pinch · tomato sauce (optional) ·

Put 2 tablespoons of the oil in a frying pan. When hot, fry the onion for 5 minutes or until it begins to brown. Add tuna and mix it well with the onion.

In another frying pan, put the remaining 3 tablespoons of oil. Add the eggs beaten with a little salt. When the eggs thicken, add the tuna mixture to the center. Fold over and serve immediately.

May be served with tomato sauce.

SERVES 2.

Tortilla de cangrejo

Crab Meat Omelet

1/2 cup canned crab meat, mashed · 3 tablespoons olive oil · 4 eggs · mayonnaise ·

Blend 1 tablespoon of the olive oil with the crab meat. Add the eggs and beat thoroughly.

Heat the remaining oil in a skillet, being sure that there is enough oil to cover the bottom of the pan. Cook the egg mixture over low heat until the bottom is crusty. Cover the pan with a plate to turn the omelet; brown the other side and serve hot.

Accompany with mayonnaise.

SERVES 3-4.

Tortilla de gamba

Shrimp Omelet

1/2 cup cooked shrimp, mashed · 3 tablespoons olive oil · 4 eggs · 1/2 teaspoon salt · mayonnaise ·

Substitute the cooked shrimp for the crab meat. Continue as in the preceding recipe, "Crab Meat Omelet" but adding salt.

Accompany with mayonnaise.

SERVES 3-4.

Tortilla de champiñones

Mushroom Omelet

1/4 pound fresh mushrooms · 4 tablespoons olive oil · 4 eggs · 1/2 teaspoon salt ·

Clean the mushrooms and slice. Heat the oil in a skillet. Sauté the mushrooms in the oil until they are soft.

Beat the eggs with salt; add to the skillet. Cook over low heat until the bottom is lightly brown. Cover the pan with a plate to turn. Brown the other side and serve hot.

SERVES 3-4.

Huevos revueltos I

Scrambled Eggs (double-boiler method)

4 eggs (or at least 2 eggs per person) · salt, to taste · 2 tablespoons cold milk · 2 tablespoons butter ·

Beat the eggs with a fork for one minute. Mix in the salt and milk. Melt 1 tablespoon of the butter in the top of a double boiler over very warm water. Add the egg mixture and cook until the eggs are thick, scraping the sides of the pan frequently. Remove from the heat. Add the additional tablespoon of butter and serve immediately.

SERVES 2.

71

Huevos revueltos II

Scrambled Eggs (skillet method)

4 eggs (or at least 2 eggs per person) · add salt, to taste · 2 tablespoons cold milk · 2 tablespoons butter ·

Beat the eggs with a fork for one minute. Mix in the salt and milk. Melt 2 tablespoons of butter in the skillet over low heat. Add the egg mixture and cook until the eggs are thick, scraping the bottom and sides of the pan frequently to keep the eggs from sticking. Serve hot.

SERVES 2.

Huevos revueltos con champiñones

Scrambled Eggs with Mushrooms

1 cup fresh mushrooms, chopped · 3 tablespoons butter · lemon juice, few drops · 3/4 teaspoon salt · 6 eggs · 3 tablespoons cream ·

Sauté the mushrooms in a skillet in the butter, lemon juice, and salt for about 10 minutes.

Beat the eggs and cream together with a fork for about 1 minute. Add to the mushroom mixture and cook until the eggs are thick, scraping the bottom and sides of pan frequently. Serve hot.

SERVES 4-6.

Huevos revueltos con jamón

Scrambled Eggs with Ham

6 eggs ·
3 tablespoons
cream or milk ·
1 cup ham,
chopped ·
3 tablespoons
butter ·

Beat the eggs with the cream for about one minute. Add the ham.

Melt the butter in a skillet; add the egg mixture and cook until the mixture is thick.

Note that no salt has been added, as most ham is quite salty. Serve hot.

SERVES 4-6.

Huevos revueltos con esparragos

Scrambled Eggs with Asparagus

6 eggs · 3
tablespoons cream
or milk · 1 cup
canned asparagus,
diced ·
1/2 teaspoon lemon
juice · 3/4 teaspoon
salt · 3 tablespoons
butter ·

Beat the eggs with the cream for about one minute. Add the asparagus, lemon juice, and salt.

Melt the butter in a skillet; add the egg mixture and cook until the mixture is thick. Serve immediately.

SERVES 4-6.

Piperade

Basque-style Scrambled Eggs

1 small green pepper · 1 small onion, chopped fine · 1 garlic clove, crushed · 3 tablespoons olive oil · 2 tomatoes, peeled and chopped · 4 eggs · 1/4 teaspoon salt · pepper, few grains ·

Remove the seeds from the green pepper and slice it very fine. Sauté the green pepper, onion, and garlic in the oil until the onion is transparent. Add the tomatoes and simmer for about 5 minutes. Break the eggs in the mixture; stir quickly to mix. Then cook slowly, stirring continually. When the mixture is firm, season with salt and pepper and serve hot.

SERVES 2-3.

Variations of Spanish Scrambled Eggs

Other adaptions for serving Spanish scrambled eggs include the following variations. Brown CHORIZO sausage, chicken livers, or shrimp in a small amount of olive oil, then proceed as in any of the basic scrambled egg recipes. For a change in the recipe for "Scrambled Eggs with Asparagus," substitute onions (for the aspragus) fried in a little olive oil until slightly brown. Also, any other vegetable like cooked and diced potatoes, cooked or canned English peas, cooked carrots, canned French-style green beans, or some leftover you find in the refrigerator may serve as a substitution.

Manera de hacer los huevos escalfados

Way of Preparing Poached Eggs

Eggs for poaching should be very fresh. If you are in doubt as to the freshness of the eggs, add 1 tablespoon of lemon juice or vinegar to each quart of water to help coagulate the egg whites.

Put the water in a pan or skillet until it is about two-thirds full. Bring the water, to which a little salt has been added, to a boil. Lower the heat. Break each egg into a cup, then carefully slip each egg into the water. Do not try to crowd the eggs, for each should remain separated from the others. Be sure the water continues to simmer; cook 3 minutes for soft-poached eggs and several minutes longer for harder yolks.

Lift the eggs carefully with a slotted spoon. Poached eggs may be served as they come from the pan with toast or English muffins, or use them with any of the poached egg recipes that follow.

Huevos escalfados con esparragos

Poached Eggs with Asparagus

2 cups canned asparagus tips · 1 tablespoon butter · 1 tablespoon olive oil · 2 tablespoons flour · 1/2 teaspoon salt · nutmeg, few grains · 1 1/2 cups milk · 6 eggs · 6 slices of toast ·

Heat the asparagus in a double boiler. Prepare a béchamel sauce by melting the butter and oil in a skillet over low heat; stir in the flour, salt, and nutmeg and blend well. Remove from the heat and gradually stir in the milk. Return to heat and stir continually until thick and smooth. Keep the sauce warm by covering the pan and placing it in hot water.

Prepare 6 poached eggs according to the directions in "Way of Preparing Poached Eggs" (page 74). Place each on a piece of buttered toast; carefully place drained asparagus tips on each egg and cover with béchamel sauce. Serve immediately.

SERVES 6.

Huevos escalfadas con champiñones

Poached Eggs with Mushrooms

**1 1/2 cups mushrooms ·
1 ounce butter or oleo · juice of 1/2 lemon ·**

FOR THE BÉCHAMEL:
**1 tablespoon butter ·
1 tablespoon olive oil · 2 tablespoons flour · 1/2 teaspoon salt ·**

6 eggs · 6 slices of toast ·

Clean and slice the mushrooms, but reserve six mushrooms whole, with the stems removed. Cook the mushrooms in the butter and lemon juice in a covered pan over low heat for 10 minutes.

Prepare the béchamel sauce according to the directions in the preceding recipe "Poached Eggs with Asparagus" but omitting the nutmeg.

Prepare the eggs following the directions for "Way of Preparing Poached Eggs" (page 74). Place some of the sliced mushrooms over each slice of toast, then add egg. Top each with a whole mushroom, and béchamel sauce. Serve immediately.

SERVES 6.

Huevos escalfados con cebollos

Poached Eggs with Onions

**2 tablespoons olive oil ·
3 medium-sized tomatoes ·
1 tablespoon sugar ·
salt, to taste · 3 medium-sized onions · flour ·
1 cup cooking oil ·
6 eggs ·**

Heat the olive oil in a skillet. Add the tomatoes that have been peeled, seeds removed, and sliced in small pieces. Mash the tomatoes as they are cooking over medium heat for 15 minutes. Force the tomatoes through a sieve; add sugar and salt. Return to low heat.

Peel and cut the onions sideways for rings, loosening each one from the other. Cover with flour and fry in hot cooking oil. Drain on paper towels.

Prepare eggs following the directions for "Way of Preparing Poached Eggs" (page 74). Place a mound of

onion rings on each plate. Top the onions with an egg and each egg with a heaping tablespoon of tomato sauce. Serve immediately.

SERVES 6.

Soufflé de queso

Cheese Soufflé

6 tablespoons butter ·
8 tablespoons flour ·
1/2 teaspoon salt ·
2 cups milk ·
1 cup cheese, grated · 4 eggs, separated ·

Melt butter in a frying pan over low heat; blend in flour and salt. Remove from heat and gradually stir in the milk. Return to heat and stir continually until thick and smooth—about 5 minutes. Add cheese and remove from the heat to blend.

Add a little of the sauce to the slightly beaten egg yolks; then stir them into the cheese sauce. Beat the egg whites until they are stiff but fluffy. Fold the whites carefully into the cheese mixture.

Pour into a 1 1/2 quart capacity greased casserole. Bake at 325° for 20 minutes; then at 425° for about 15 minutes or until soufflé is raised and golden brown on top. Serve immediately or it will drop.

SERVES 6.

Soufflé de patata

Potato Soufflé

2 1/2 pounds potatoes, peeled · 4 tablespoons butter · 1 cup milk, heated · 4 eggs, separated · nutmeg, few grains · salt, a pinch ·

Cut the potatoes in large slices. Boil them in salted water for 20 to 30 minutes, or until they are very tender when pierced with a knife. Drain and force through a sieve. Dot with half (2 tablespoons) of the butter. Slowly add the hot milk, stirring with a wooden spoon.

Grease a 1 1/2 quart casserole with the remaining butter. Stir the slightly beaten egg yolks into the potato mixture with the nutmeg and salt. Beat the egg whites until they are stiff but fluffy. Fold the whites carefully into the potato mixture.

Pile lightly into the casserole. Bake in a preheated hot oven (425°) about 25-30 minutes. The soufflé should be raised and golden brown. Serve immediately from the casserole dish.

SERVES 6.

Manera de hacer los huevos fritos

Way of Preparing Fried Eggs

Do not fry more than 2 eggs at a time. Heat 3 tablespoons of olive oil, vegetable oil, or bacon drippings in a frying pan over moderate heat. Break the egg in a cup and slip it into the pan. Baste the egg occasionally with the fat using a spatula. You may prefer to turn the egg after it is partially set and cook it for a moment on the other side until firm.

Remove and serve on individual plates with salt and pepper.

Huevos fritos en bollos

Fried Eggs in Muffins

FOR THE SAUCE:
1 1/2 tablespoons oil or bacon grease ·
2 medium-sized tomatoes ·
1 tablespoon sugar ·
1/2 teaspoon salt ·

3 English muffins ·
6 egg yolks · 4 egg whites · salt ·
4 cups oil ·

Heat the fat in a skillet. Add the tomatoes (that have been peeled, seeds removed, and cut in small pieces), sugar, and salt. Cook over medium heat for 15 minutes; (the mixture should be rather thick) then force the tomatoes through a sieve. Return to low heat to keep warm.

Split each muffin in two. Remove a little of the muffin to make a hole for the egg. Put a yolk in each muffin. Salt lightly. Beat the egg whites until very firm. Place a little of the tomato sauce around each egg yolk. Top with egg whites.

Deep fat fry the eggs very rapidly in medium hot oil holding them with a slotted spoon or sieve. Or you may prefer to bake the eggs in a 350° oven 12 to 15 minutes until the egg whites begin to brown.

SERVES 6.

Huevos fritos con arroz

Fried Eggs with Rice

FOR THE SAUCE:
3 tablespoons bacon grease ·
3 medium-sized tomatoes ·
1 tablespoon sugar ·
1/2 teaspoon salt ·

3 cups cooked rice ·
6 slices of bacon, crumbled · 6 eggs ·
salt, to taste ·

Heat the fat in a skillet. Continue to prepare the sauce by following the preceding recipe "Fried Eggs in Muffins."

Prepare rice according to directions on package. Fry the bacon until crisp; drain and crumble into pieces.

On a serving platter or on individual plates, form a mound of rice in the shape of a crown. Fill the center of each with tomato sauce. Garnish the rice with the pieces of bacon.

Fry the eggs (you may have to add more bacon grease

or oil). Put a fried egg in each mound of rice. Serve immediately.

SERVES 6.

Huevos pasados por agua

Soft-boiled Eggs

Put enough water in a pan to cover not more than 6 eggs at a time. Add 1 tablespoon of salt and bring the water to a boil. Carefully lower each egg into the water on a spoon to keep the shell from cracking. Reduce the heat and simmer 3 minutes for a soft-boiled egg. Serve in an egg cup or coffee cup with toast.

Manera de hacer los huevos duros

Way of Preparing Hard-boiled Eggs

Put enough water in the pan to cover all of the eggs that you are going to prepare. Bring to a boil and add 1 tablespoon of salt for every 4 eggs. Carefully lower each egg in the water on a spoon. Reduce the heat to simmer. Occasionally move the eggs around with a wooden spoon so that the yolk remains in the center of the egg. Allow 12 minutes of cooking time for medium eggs and 15 minutes for large eggs. Replace the hot water with cold water; let the eggs stay in the water until you are ready to use them.

Huevos duros con gambas

Hard-boiled Eggs with Shrimp

1 pound shrimp, fresh or frozen · 1/2 celery stalk, chopped · 1/4 cup onion, chopped · 1 teaspoon salt · 9 eggs ·

FOR THE SAUCE: 3 tablespoons olive oil · 1 medium onion, peeled and chopped · 3 tablespoons flour · 1/3 cup white wine · 1 1/2 cups water used for cooking the shrimp · salt, to taste ·

If you are using frozen shrimp, prepare according to the directions on the package. For fresh shrimp, bring 3 cups of water to boil with the celery, onion, and salt. Add the shrimp; bring to a second boil; remove from the heat and let stand 6 to 8 minutes. Pour off the water but reserve it; cool and remove shells.

Cook the eggs according to the preceding directions for "Way of Preparing Hard-boiled Eggs." Shell and cut each egg in half lengthwise. Remove and reserve the yolks.

For the sauce: Heat the oil in a skillet; fry the onion until it begins to brown (about 8 minutes). Add the flour and stir with a wooden spoon. Slowly add the wine; then the water, stirring continually for 5 minutes. Force through a sieve. Add salt. Return to very low heat so the mixture will stay hot.

Mix 7 of the egg yolks with the shrimp. Place the egg whites on an oven-proof platter. You may have to cut a little piece from the bottom of the egg so it will be level and won't slide. Mix several tablespoons of sauce with the shrimp and fill each egg.

Bake in a 325° preheated oven for about 10 minutes. Garnish with the 3 remaining yolks, which have been mashed with a fork, and serve immediately.

SERVES 6.

Huevos duros con anchoas

Hard-boiled Eggs with Anchovies

9 eggs · 6 canned anchovies · 1 tablespoon parsley, chopped · 1 tablespoon butter · lemon juice, few drops ·

FOR THE BÉCHAMEL: 1 tablespoon butter · 2 tablespoons olive oil · 3 tablespoons flour · 1 1/2 cups cold milk · salt and pepper, to taste · 3 tablespoons cheese, grated

Prepare the eggs according to the directions for "Way of Preparing Hard-boiled Eggs" (page 80). Shell and cut each egg in half lengthwise. Remove the yolks. Cut a very thin strip from the bottom of the egg white and place on an oven-proof platter.

Drain the oil from the anchovies; chop them; mix them with the egg yolks, the butter (should be soft) and the lemon juice. Fill each egg.

Prepare a béchamel sauce by melting the butter over low heat. Add oil, and blend in the flour. Gradually stir in the milk. Cook, stirring constantly, until thick and smooth. Add salt and pepper. Pour the béchamel over the eggs.

Top with grated cheese and bake in a 325° preheated oven about 10 minutes or until the béchamel begins to brown. Serve immediately.

SERVES 6.

los platos con arroz y los caceroles

6

rice dishes and casseroles

By far the most famous rice dish in Spain today is PAELLA. Look in a Spanish-English dictionary and you will find that it is a saffron-flavored dish of rice with seafood, meat, chicken, and various vegetables. The name probably originated from the large, heavy iron skillet, which is rather shallow and has two flattened handles, always used by the Spanish cooks to prepare the paella. Undoubtedly, the dish originated along the banks and lagoons near Valencia on the Mediterranean coast of Spain where much of the country's rice has been grown since the time of the Moors. Although paella used to be more popular along coastal towns, now it is possible to order paella nearly everywhere in Spain.

When preparing this dish at home, you may have to make some substitutions depending on what is available in your area of the United States. Saffron is available in most gourmet stores, but very expensive although well worth the investment.

Paella a la Valenciana

Valencia-style Paella

Paella is served in the pan in which it is cooked, called the PAELLERA, along with the shells from the clams.

1/4 cup olive oil · 1-3 garlic cloves, crushed · 1-3 pound chicken, cut into serving pieces · 3 medium-sized tomatoes, peeled and chopped · 1 medium-sized onion, chopped · 1 large red pepper, seeded and cut in strips · 1 teaspoon paprika · salt and pepper, to taste · 2 cups medium or long-grain rice, uncooked · 1/4 teaspoon powdered saffron · 4 cups chicken broth or stock · 1 pound raw shrimp, peeled · 1 cup green peas, fresh or frozen · 12 fresh clams, cleaned and scrubbed (optional) · 1 lemon, cut into slices for garnish ·

Heat oil in a heavy iron skillet (unless you have a paella pan). Add garlic to flavor.

NOTICE: you may use from 1 to 3 cloves, and you may prefer to cook the garlic for a few minutes and remove before adding the other ingredients.

Add chicken, tomatoes, onion, and red pepper. Coat the mixture with the oil. Sprinkle with paprika, salt, and pepper. Cook over low heat for 10-12 minutes, stirring occasionally. Increase the heat to medium; add rice and stir constantly until the rice begins to brown. Shake the pan frequently.

In a separate pan, bring the chicken broth or stock to boil with the saffron. Pour the liquid into the rice mixture and stir quickly to combine. Bring to boil; reduce heat and simmer 15 to 20 minutes. Most of the liquid should be absorbed. Add shrimp, peas, and clams. If you are using clams, push them under the rice to cook. Cover and cook about 15 minutes until the clam shells have opened. Be sure to DISCARD any shells that do not open. Place the lemon slices around the edge of the pan for garnish.

Serve immediately.

SERVES 6-8.

Paella a la Nueva York

New York-style Paella

1/3 cup olive oil · 1 small chicken, cut into serving pieces · 2 large pork sausages · 1/2 cup ham, diced · 1 medium onion, chopped · 1 green pepper, chopped · 1 teaspoon oregano · 1/4 teaspoon garlic powder · 1/4 teaspoon powdered saffron · 1 teaspoon salt · 1/4 teaspoon pepper · 1 1/2 cups medium or long-grain rice, uncooked · 1 can (8 oz.) tomato sauce · 3 cups boiling water · 1 small lobster, cooked and cut up with shell · 1/2 cup green peas, fresh or frozen · 1/2 cup corn, fresh or frozen whole kernel · 8 fresh small clams (optional) · 1 can (4 oz.) pimientos, cut up for garnish ·

Heat oil in a heavy iron skillet. Lightly brown the chicken. Blend in the sausages, ham, onion, and green pepper. Reduce heat to low.

Stir in oregano, garlic powder, saffron, salt, pepper, and the uncooked rice. Add the tomato sauce and boiling water. Cover and simmer 20 minutes. Stir in lobster, peas, and corn; cover and simmer another 10 minutes.

If you are adding clams, place them in cold water for 5 to 10 minutes. Clean and scrub the clams to remove all sand. Steam the clams in a little water in a small saucepan until the shells open—about 15 minutes. Be sure to DISCARD any shells that do not open.

You may prefer to serve this paella on a large platter. Garnish with clams and their shells and pieces of pimiento.

SERVES 6.

Variations of Paella

Paella can be considered a Spanish stew. Just like stews in our country, there are many variations depending on the availability of the ingredients. You will notice though that paella is a mixture of both meat and seafood. Also, two necessary ingredients are saffron and medium or long-grain rice.

Follow the preceeding recipe for "New York-style Paella."

VARIATION 1   Substitute 1/4 pound salami and 1/2 pound of shrimp for the sausage and ham.

VARIATION 2   Substitute 1/4 pound diced pork, 3 lobster tails, and 1/2 pound of clams for the ham, lobster pieces, and 8 small clams.

VARIATION 3   Substitute 3 diced chicken breasts and 1 pound shelled shrimp for the servings of chicken and lobster.

Different vegetables may be used:

Follow the preceding recipe for "New York-style Paella."

VARIATION 1   Substitute artichoke hearts and green beans for the green peas and corn.

VARIATION 2   Substitute lima beans for the corn.

VARIATION 3   Substitute green beans for the green peas.

Arroz de Sevilla

Seville-style Rice

1 cup uncooked rice · 1 onion, finely chopped · 1 celery stalk, chopped · 1 medium-size green pepper, chopped · 1/2 cup fresh mushrooms, sliced · 1/2 teaspoon rosemary · 1/2 teaspoon basil · 2 tablespoons olive oil · 1 tablespoon bacon drippings · 1 cup (8 oz.) stewed tomatoes · 1 can (10-1/2 ounce) beef broth · 1/4 cup stuffed green olives, sliced

Sauté rice, onion, celery, green pepper, mushrooms, rosemary, and basil in the oil and bacon drippings until the vegetables are tender.

Drain stewed tomatoes, reserving liquid. Add enough of the tomato liquid to the beef broth to equal 2 cups. Water may have to be added.

Add liquid, tomatoes, and olives to the rice mixture. Cover and simmer 20 minutes.

SERVES 6.

Pilaf de arroz

Rice Pilaf

2 tablespoons olive oil · 1 cup uncooked rice · 1/2 cup onion, chopped · 3/4 teaspoon salt · 1/8 teaspoon pepper · 1/2 teaspoon oregano · 1 3/4 cups water · 2 beef bouillon cubes · 1 tablespoon olive oil · 1/3 cup almonds, blanched and slivered · 1 tablespoon parsley, chopped ·

Heat 2 tablespoons olive oil in a 2-quart saucepan. Add rice. Stir constantly until rice is golden brown. Add onion, salt, pepper, oregano, water, and bouillon cubes. When cubes are dissolved, cover and simmer over low heat 20 minutes or until rice is tender and liquid is absorbed. Heat 1 tablespoon olive oil in a small saucepan. Stir in almonds and sauté until lightly browned. Stir almonds and parsley into rice.

SERVES 6.

Arroz blanco

White Rice

For any recipe calling for plain white rice, here is a good basic recipe. Both medium or long-grain domestic rice work well for these recipes. If you are using imported, use the short-grain variety. The Spanish cooks will tell you not to use rice grown in Calasparra for it is not as tender; so I shall warn you NOT to buy rice from Calasparra.

1 cup uncooked rice · 2 quarts (8 cups) water · 2 teaspoons salt · 1/4 teaspoon lemon juice · 2 tablespoons butter ·

Wash the rice, if necessary, by placing it in a sieve or colander under running water. The rice is clean when the water comes out clear.

Slowly add the rice to the boiling water to which the salt and lemon juice has been added. These acids help the rice stay white and separated. Boil gently for

15 to 20 minutes. The rice should be tender. Cooking time depends on the type of rice used.

Drain in a sieve or colander. Stir in the butter. Keep hot until ready to use.

NOTE: For yellow rice as in the paella recipes, add 1/3 teaspoon of powdered saffron while the 1 cup of rice is cooking.

SERVES 6 1/2-CUP SERVINGS.

Arroz blanco con champiñones

White Rice with Mushrooms

1 cup of uncooked rice · 2 quarts (8 cups) water · 3 teaspoons salt · few drops lemon juice or vinegar (optional) · 1 pound fresh mushrooms · 1/8 cup butter · 1/8 cup olive oil · salt · 1/4 cup flour · 2 1/2 cups milk · 2 egg yolks ·

Prepare the rice according to the preceding directions for "White Rice." Keep hot in a colander or sieve.

Clean the mushrooms and slice them in several slices. Sauté the mushrooms in the butter and oil with a few drops of lemon juice and salt. Cover and cook for 10 minutes, stirring occasionally. Blend in the flour. Remove from heat.

Stir in the milk gradually. Add more salt if necessary. Cook over low heat until the mixture is smooth, about 10 minutes. Beat the egg yolks in a cup and add them to the sauce. Heat again, but do not boil.

Arrange the rice around the edge of a serving dish. Put the mushroom sauce in the center and serve immediately.

SERVES 6.

90

Arroz blanco con pechugas de gallina y champiñones

White Rice with Chicken Breasts and Mushrooms

2 chicken breasts ·
1 small scallion (or
onion), cut in half ·
1 carrot, sliced ·
1/2 bay leaf · salt, to
taste ·

Cook the chicken breasts in enough water to cover with the white part of the scallion cut in half, the carrot, bay leaf, and salt to taste. Cook over medium heat about 45 minutes, or until the chicken is very tender. Debone, slice and set aside.

FOR THE RICE:
1 cup uncooked rice ·
8 cups water ·
3 teaspoons salt ·
2 tablespoons
butter ·

Prepare the rice according to the directions for "White Rice" on page 89.

Sauté the mushrooms in the oil. Cover and cook for 10 minutes, stirring occasionally.

1/2 pound
mushrooms,
cleaned and sliced ·
2 tablespoons olive
oil ·

In a separate skillet, melt the butter with the oil. Blend in the flour. Slowly add the milk alternating with the chicken broth. Add salt to taste; cook over low heat about 15 minutes until the mixture is smooth. Beat the egg yolks in a cup and add to the sauce. Do not allow the sauce to boil.

FOR THE SAUCE:
2 tablespoons
butter ·
2 tablespoons olive
oil · 4 tablespoons
flour · 1 cup milk ·
1 1/2 cups chicken
broth · salt, to
taste · 2 egg yolks ·

Add the mushrooms with their juice and the sliced chicken to the sauce.

Arrange the rice around the edge of a serving dish. Place the chicken-mushroom sauce in the center and serve immediately.

SERVES 6.

Arroz amarillo con huevos revueltos

Yellow Rice with Scrambled Eggs

1 cup rice,
uncooked · 8 cups
water · 2 teaspoons
salt · 1/3 teaspoon
powdered saffron ·
2 tablespoons
butter ·
1 (8 1/2 oz.) can
green peas ·
1 tablespoon
butter · 8 eggs ·
3 tablespoons
milk · 1/2 pound
shrimp, cooked and
chopped (optional)·

Prepare the rice according to the recipe for "White Rice" on page 89, but add the saffron according to the NOTE at the bottom of the recipe. Add the peas.

Melt the butter in the top of a double boiler. Add the eggs beaten with the milk. When the eggs begin to thicken, add the shrimp. Continue to cook, scraping the sides of the pan frequently until the eggs are creamy.

Place the rice and peas on half of a platter. Put the scrambled eggs on the other half and serve immediately.

SERVES 6.

Macarrones con chorizo y tomate

Macaroni with Sausage and Tomato Sauce

FOR THE SAUCE:
3 tablespoons olive
oil or other fat ·
1 medium-sized
onion, chopped ·
3 large tomatoes,
peeled and sliced ·
1 tablespoon sugar ·
1/4 teaspoon salt ·

2 cups macaroni,
uncooked ·
4 ounces Gruyère
or Parmesan
cheese, grated ·
4 ounces chorizo
sausage, or
pepperoni ·
2 tablespoons
butter ·

Heat the fat in a skillet. Sauté the onion until it is transparent, about 5 minutes. Add the tomatoes; cook over medium heat about 15 minutes. Pass the sauce through a colander. Add sugar and salt and set aside.

Prepare the macaroni according to the directions on the package. Drain. Mix the tomato sauce and cheese with the macaroni in a buttered 1 1/2 quart casserole dish; reserve several tablespoons of sauce and a little cheese for topping.

Remove the peeling from the sausage and slice. Mix with the macaroni. Top with the remaining tomato sauce and cheese. Dot with butter. Bake in 325° preheated oven about 20 minutes.

SERVES 6.

93

Macarrones con Béchamel

Macaroni with Béchamel Sauce

2 cups macaroni, uncooked · 2 tablespoons butter · 1 tablespoon olive oil · 3 tablespoons flour · salt and pepper, to taste · 2 cups cold milk · nutmeg, pinch (optional) · 1/2 cup Gruyère or Parmesan cheese, grated · butter ·

Cook the macaroni according to the directions on the package. Drain and set aside.

Prepare the sauce by melting the butter in a frying pan; add oil; blend in flour, salt, and pepper. Remove from heat. Gradually stir in the cold milk. Return to low heat and stir constantly until thick and smooth—10 minutes or more.

Mix the macaroni with 2/3 of the sauce, the nutmeg and 1/2 of the cheese in a buttered 1 1/2 quart casserole dish. Top with the remaining sauce and cheese. Dot with butter.

Bake in 325° preheated oven about 20-30 minutes or until a crust forms.

SERVES 6.

Macarrones a la americana

American-style Macaroni

The name AMERICAN-STYLE may be misleading, but this is the term used by the Spanish cooks because they always prepare this dish with Campbell's brand of soup. However, you can see that this macaroni casserole has a distinct Spanish flare.

2 cups macaroni, uncooked · 2 cans Campbell's cream of mushroom soup · 1 1/2 cups milk ·

Cook the macaroni according to the directions on the package. Drain and set aside.

Slowly mix the milk with the soup over low heat. Add the macaroni and sprinkle with curry powder. Mix

94

1/2 teaspoon curry powder · 1/4 cup Gruyère or Parmesan cheese, grated · butter ·

well; put in a buttered baking dish. Top with cheese and dot with butter.

Bake in 325° preheated oven about 15 minutes and serve hot.

SERVES 6.

Cacerola de bernejena española y macarrones

Spanish Eggplant and Macaroni Casserole

1/2 cup olive oil · 8 Italian sweet sausages · 2 cloves garlic, crushed · 1 cup onion, chopped · 2 medium eggplants, peeled and chopped · 2 teaspoons salt · 1 teaspoon paprika · 1 can (28 oz.) tomatoes with liquid · 1 can (6 oz.) tomato paste · 1/2 teaspoon sugar · 1/4 cup water · 1/4 tablespoon oregano · 2 cups macaroni, cooked according to directions on package · 1 package (16 oz.) Mozzarella cheese, slices · 1 pound Ricotta cheese · 1/4 cup Parmesan cheese, grated · chopped parsley ·

Heat olive oil in a large saucepan; cut sausages into small pieces; add to oil with garlic; cook 10 minutes or until well done. Stir in onion and eggplant; cook until tender. Add salt, paprika, tomatoes, tomato paste, sugar, water, and oregano. Stir well.

Cook over medium heat 15 minutes or until slightly thickened. Stir in macaroni. Spoon half of mixture into a 6-quart casserole. Arrange half the Mozzarella and half the Ricotta over macaroni. Repeat layers. Bake at 350° for 30 minutes. Sprinkle with Parmesan cheese and parsley.

SERVES 8-10.

Spaghettis a la italiana con bacón y huevos

Italian-style Spaghetti with Bacon and Eggs

8-9 ounces spaghetti · 1/2 pound bacon · 2 tablespoons butter · 4 eggs, beaten · Italian herb seasoning, a pinch · 1/3 cup Parmesan cheese, grated · salt and pepper, to taste ·

Cook the spaghetti according to the directions on the package. Drain and keep warm.

Cut the bacon in 4-inch strips and fry. Melt the butter in a large pot; add the fried bacon and the eggs. Mix in the spaghetti, herb seasoning, and cheese. Add salt and pepper to taste.

Mix thoroughly and heat at 325° for 15 minutes.

SERVES 6.

Spaghettis con guisantes y almejas

Spaghetti with Peas and Clams

8-9 ounces of spaghetti · 18 clams · 1/2 cup white wine · 1 medium onion, finely chopped · 2 ounces butter · 1/2 cup canned green peas · salt and pepper, to taste · 1/3 cup Parmesan cheese, grated ·

Cook the spaghetti according to the directions on the package. Drain in a colander.

Clean and scrub the clams to remove all sand. While the spaghetti is cooking, put the clams in a frying pan with the wine and onion. Cook over low heat, shaking the pan from time to time until the clams open. DIS-CARD any shells that do not open. Remove the clams from their shells; strain the liquid that is in the frying pan through a colander or piece of gauze to remove any sand.

Melt the butter and pour in a casserole dish. Mix in the spaghetti, clams, peas, and the strained liquid. Season with salt and pepper. Top with Parmesan cheese.

Heat in a 325° oven for 20 minutes and serve hot.

SERVES 6.

Cacerola de carne picada y española

Spanish Ground Beef Casserole

1 pound ground lean beef · 2 tablespoons olive oil · 1/2 cup onion, chopped · 1 clove garlic, crushed · few drops hot pepper sauce · 1 can (16 oz.) tomatoes with liquid · 1/2 cup dry white wine · 1/2 cup stuffed olives, sliced · 1/2 teaspoon salt · 1/2 teaspoon cumin · dash black pepper · 3 cups cooked rice ·

Brown meat in olive oil. Add onion and garlic; cook until tender but not browned. Stir in remaining ingredients. Pour in 2-quart casserole. Bake at 350° for 30 minutes.

SERVES 6.

los pescados y los mariscos
7
fish and shellfish

As the Iberian Peninsula is surrounded by water on three sides, it is no wonder that PESCADOS (fish) and MARISCOS (shellfish) are in abundance. Although the recipes in this chapter are authentic, as they all originated in Spain, it is almost impossible to duplicate some famous Spanish seafood dishes in the United States. In the Basque provinces, a delicacy is "hake's throat," which is a casserole of parsley, peas, and garlic. Equally famous and delicious are baby eels cooked in boiling oil with chilies, and another favorite is squid simmered in its own ink. The secret to the wonderful taste is that seafood served in Spain is fresh.

Merluza tropical

Fish Steaks Tropical

1 1/2 pounds hake, halibut, or haddock steaks · 2 teaspoons lemon juice · 1 teaspoon salt · 1/4 cup olive oil · 4 small bananas · 1/3 cup blanched almonds, chopped · 1 tablespoon onion, chopped · 1/4 cup seedless raisins · 1 tablespoon parsley, minced · 1 can (8 1/2 oz.) pineapple chunks, drained · 1/4 cup water · 1/4 cup sherry ·

Cut fish into serving pieces. Sprinkle with lemon juice and salt. Heat the oil in a skillet. Sauté fish gently on each side until they begin to brown. Place them in a shallow baking dish.

Peel bananas and slice lengthwise. Sauté in the oil in the skillet until lightly brown. Place the bananas around the fish. Add nuts and onion to skillet. Cook 1 minute. Then stir in the raisins, parsley, pineapple, water, and sherry. Pour this mixture over the fish in the baking dish.

Bake at 325° for 15 minutes.

NOTE: Merluza is hake, but as this species of fish is unavailable in many parts of the United States, recipes calling for hake will offer substitutes.

SERVES 4.

Merluza a la marinera

Hake Fillets in Tomato and Almond Sauce

3 tablespoons olive oil · 1 small onion, chopped · 2 garlic cloves, crushed · 1/2 cup almonds, ground · 1/4 cup fresh breadcrumbs · 4 tablespoons parsley, chopped · 4 medium-sized tomatoes, peeled, seeded and finely chopped ·

2 pounds hake fillets (or substitute haddock or other white fish) · 3 cups hot water · juice of 1/2 lemon · 1/2 teaspoon salt · 2 tablespoons slivered almonds ·

Heat the oil over medium heat in a large frying pan. Add the onion and garlic and fry until they are soft. Remove the pan from the heat and stir in the ground almonds, breadcrumbs, 3 tablespoons of the parsley, and the tomatoes. Return to the heat and cook for 5 minutes, or until the liquid has evaporated and the mixture is thick.

Wipe fillets with a clean wet cloth and arrange them in one layer in a large, shallow baking dish. Pour water, lemon juice, and salt over them. Cover the dish with foil and bake in a preheated 350° oven for 25 minutes, or until the fish flakes easily when prodded gently with a fork. Carefully transfer the fillets to a warm serving platter.

Strain and reserve 1/2 cup of the liquid in which the fish cooked. Add this to the tomato and almond mixture in the frying pan. Stir well to blend. Cook over medium heat until the mixture is smooth, stirring continually. Taste for seasoning. You may need to add more salt. Pour the sauce over the fish and garnish with the slivered almonds and remaining parsley. Serve at once.

SERVES 6.

102

Merluza en salsa verde

Hake in Green Sauce

4 tablespoons olive oil · 1 medium-sized onion · 1 garlic clove, minced · parsley, several sprigs · salt, a pinch · 1 tablespoon flour · 1 cup cold water ·

6 thick slices of hake or other white fish · 1 small can green peas · black pepper, few grains · 2 hard-boiled eggs, chopped (optional) ·

Heat the oil in a frying pan. Fry the onion. While the onion is frying, crush the minced garlic with the parsley in a mortar and pestle or in a food processor; sprinkle with salt. When the onion is transparent (about 5 minutes), stir in the flour and slowly add the water. Remove a couple of tablespoons of this mixture and mix with the mashed garlic and parsley. Add this to the sauce in the frying pan. Mix well. Strain the sauce through a large-holed colander into a heat resistant casserole.

Arrange the fish slices, lightly salted, in the casserole. The sauce should just cover them. You may have to add more water. Shake the dish to blend the sauce. Add the peas and pepper. Cover dish and cook over low heat 25-30 minutes or until the fish flakes easily when tested with a fork. Shake the dish periodically to thicken the sauce; add more salt if necessary.

Serve immediately from the casserole, garnishing the dish with parsley and chopped eggs, if you wish.

SERVES 6.

Merluza al horno con tomates y queso rallado

Baked Hake with Tomatoes and Grated Cheese

3 1/2 to 4 pounds hake or other white fish · salt · 2 tablespoons butter · 1 cup Gruyère or Parmesan cheese, grated · 4 medium-sized tomatoes, peeled ·

Have the backbone of the fish removed at the market. Wash the fish and dry with a paper towel. Sprinkle the cavity with salt. Add 1 tablespoon of the butter and half of the cheese. Close the cavity with toothpicks or skewers.

Cut the tomatoes in half and place them in the center of a baking dish. Set aside 3 of the halves. Salt the tomatoes and place the fish on top of them. Cover the fish with the remaining butter, tomatoes and grated cheese. Bake in a 350° preheated oven for 30-40 minutes or until the fish is a golden color. Serve at once.

SERVES 6.

Filetes fritos de merluza

Fried Hake Fillets

3 pounds hake or other white fish fillets · 3 cups oil · 2 eggs, beaten · 1 1/2 cups of flour · salt and pepper, to taste · 1 lemon, sliced in 6 pieces ·

Wash and cut the fish into serving pieces.

Heat the oil in a frying pan over moderate heat. The oil should be hot but not smoking. Dip each fillet in egg, then in flour, to which salt and pepper have been added. Flour both sides of the fillet and shake off any excess flour.

Fry until brown; then turn to brown other side. Reduce heat and cook slowly until fish are thoroughly cooked.

Drain on paper towels. Serve on a platter garnished with slices of lemon.

SERVES 6.

Rodajas de merluza al horno
con salsa de crema y champiñones

Baked Hake Steaks
with Mushroom and Cream Sauce

3 tablespoons olive oil · 6 hake or other white fish steaks · salt · 3/4 cup white wine · 1 1/2 lemons · 4 sprigs parsley · 2 tablespoons bread crumbs · butter · 1/3 pound fresh mushrooms · 1/2 pint heavy cream ·

Put the oil in a baking dish. Wash the fish steaks and dry them with paper towels. Salt both sides and arrange them in the greased baking dish. Pour the wine mixed with the juice of 1 lemon over the fish. Put a sprig of parsley between each steak. Top each steak with some bread crumbs and butter. Bake in a 350° preheated oven about 30 minutes or until the steaks are a golden color, and the fish flakes easily when tested with a fork.

While the fish is baking, clean and slice the mushrooms. Sauté the mushrooms in a skillet with butter and the remaining juice of 1/2 lemon. Cover and cook for 10 minutes over moderate heat. Lower the heat; add the cream. Stir until well blended.

Remove the sprigs of parsley from the baking dish. Cover the fish with the mushroom sauce. Heat in the oven for 5 more minutes and serve hot from the baking dish.

SERVES 6.

Filete de lenguado con béchamel

Fillet of Sole with Béchamel Sauce

2 pounds fillet of sole · 1 cup fish stock · 1 teaspoon onion, grated · curry powder, pinch · 1 tablespoon butter · 1 tablespoon olive oil · 2 tablespoons flour · 1 cup sour cream · salt and pepper, to taste · 1/4 cup cheese, grated ·

Wash the fillets and dry them on paper towels. Cut in serving pieces unless they are small. Add salt to taste, and put them in a shallow baking dish.

Fish stock is made by placing the head, tail, bones and fins in a pan with 2 cups of water (or enough to cover) and 1 teaspoon of salt. Cover and simmer 30-40 minutes. Strain before using.

Prepare the béchamel by simmering together the fish stock, onion, and curry powder for 15 minutes. Strain and reserve 1 cup.

Melt the butter over low heat; add the oil, and blend in the flour. Remove from the heat and blend in the sour cream and fish stock. Return to heat and stir continually until smooth. Season with salt and pepper.

Pour the sauce over the fillets. Top with Gruyère or other grated cheese.

Bake at 375° for 20-25 minutes or until the fillets flake easily when tested with a fork.

SERVES 6.

Filete de lenguado al horno con vino blanco

Fillet of Sole with White Wine

**2 pounds fillet of
sole · salt, to taste ·
1/2 cup olive oil ·
1/2 cup white wine ·
1 small onion,
chopped ·
1 tablespoon
parsley, finely
chopped ·
all-purpose
seasoning, a pinch
or two · 1 cup fish
stock (refer to
preceding recipe
for preparation of
fish stock) ·**

Wash the fillets. Cut them in serving pieces unless they are small; add salt to taste and arrange them in an oiled shallow baking dish side-by-side. Sprinkle with the rest of the olive oil and white wine.

Mix together the onion, parsley, and all-purpose seasoning. Arrange on top of the fish. Pour the fish stock around the edge of the baking dish. Shake the dish so the liquid is evenly distributed.

Bake in a preheated oven at 375° for 20-25 minutes or until the fillets flake easily when tested with a fork.

SERVES 6.

Caldo corto con vino blanco

Broth with White Wine

Many of the fish recipes call for "Caldo Corto." This is a broth that may be made up ahead of time and refrigerated for several days before using.

**2 cups cold water ·
1 bay leaf · 1 small
onion, sliced ·
1 large carrot,
scraped and cut in
small round pieces ·
1 cup white wine ·
juice of 1/2 lemon ·
salt, to taste ·**

Simmer all of the ingredients together for 20 minutes. Strain. Allow to cool thoroughly before using.

ENOUGH BROTH FOR COATING 2 POUNDS OF FISH.

107

Filete de lenguado con arroz

Fillet of Sole with Rice

broth with white wine · 2 pounds fillet of sole · white rice (page 89) · 1/2 pound fresh mushrooms · 2 tablespoons butter · juice of 1/2 lemon · add salt, to taste · 1/2 cup cooked ham, chopped ·

FOR THE SAUCE: 2 tablespoons olive oil · 2 tablespoons flour · 1 cup cold milk · 1/2 cup broth · salt and pepper, to taste ·

Prepare the broth according to the preceding recipe the day before, and refrigerate.

Put the fillets in the cold broth. Bring to a full boil. Turn off the heat and let the fish continue to cook in the hot broth.

Meanwhile prepare the white rice. Put it in the center of a platter and keep warm.

Clean and slice the mushrooms. Sauté the mushrooms in the butter, lemon juice, and salt to taste. Cook over low heat for 10 minutes; add ham.

Prepare a sauce by heating the oil and blending in the flour. Slowly add the cold milk; cook for 5 minutes over low heat stirring continually. Add 1/2 cup of broth in which the fish cooked. Add salt and pepper to taste.

Arrange the fillets around the rice. Cover the fillets with mushroom and ham mixture; then add the sauce. Serve immediately.

SERVES 6.

Truchas fritas

Fried Trout

12 trout, about 6 oz. each · salt · 3/4 cup milk · 1 1/4 cups flour · salt and pepper, to taste · oil for frying · lemon slices ·

Clean and dry the fish. Salt the cavity and also the outside of the trout. Set aside for 10 minutes to allow the salt to penetrate. Dip each fish in milk, then in flour that has been seasoned with salt and pepper.

Fry in deep hot oil (360° to 370° or until a crust of bread will brown in 1 minute) for about 10 minutes. Serve with lemon slices.

For a little variety, dip the fish in flour first. Then, dip in well-beaten eggs and then in bread crumbs. Fry for 10 minutes and also serve with slices of lemon.

SERVES 6.

Truchas a la molinera

Miller's Wife-style of Trout

12 trout · salt, to taste · 1 cup cold milk · 1 1/2 cups flour · 4 ounces butter · juice of 1 lemon · 1 tablespoon parsley ·

Fry the fish according to the preceding recipe for "Fried Trout." Place the trout on a serving platter in the oven either on low heat (300°) or in a hot oven in which the heat has been turned off.

In a small pan, melt the butter; remove from heat; add the lemon juice.

Pour the butter mixed with the lemon juice over the fish. Sprinkle with parsley and serve immediately.

NOTE: To get the maximum amount of juice from a lemon, be sure it is at room temperature and not cold.

SERVES 6.

Bacalao al ajo arriero

Codfish in Garlic Sauce

1 pound of salt codfish, shredded · 4 tablespoons olive oil · 1 large onion, finely chopped · 6 pimientos, chopped · 2-3 cloves garlic, finely chopped · 5 medium-sized tomatoes, peeled, seeded, and chopped ·

Starting the day before you plan to serve the codfish, tear them into pieces as fine as possible and soak in enough water to cover overnight. (If you are using packaged shredded codfish, follow the directions on the package.) Dry the fish with paper towels.

In a heavy skillet heat 2 tablespoons of the oil and cook the fish in the oil over moderate heat until golden. Drain on paper towels.

Add the remaining 2 tablespoons of oil to the skillet and cook the onion, pimientos, and garlic until the onion is tender. Add the tomatoes. Bring to a boil; lower heat and cook about 20 minutes.

Return the fish to the skillet; cover and simmer over low heat for 15 minutes. Remove from the heat and set aside, still covered, for about 15 minutes before serving.

SERVES 6.

Fritos de bacalao

Fried Codfish Balls

2 pounds potatoes · 1 pound salt codfish · 1 garlic clove, chopped · 1 tablespoon parsley, chopped · 2 egg yolks · 2 egg whites · oil for frying ·

Wash the unpeeled potatoes and put them in cold water to cover with the salt codfish. Bring to a boil and cook about 30 minutes or until the potatoes and fish are very tender. Drain. Be sure all skin and bones are removed from the fish. Peel the potatoes and mash them with the fish.

Mix the garlic, parsley, and egg yolks, which have been slightly beaten, with the potatoes and fish. Beat the egg whites nearly stiff and mix gently with the fish mixture. Refrigerate to cool.

110

Shape into balls. Fry in hot oil (about 375°) until browned. Drain on paper towels and serve hot with Granada sauce (page 35), Romesco sauce (page 39), or Italian-style sauce (page 41).

SERVES 6.

Bacalao en salsa verde

Codfish in Green Sauce

2 pounds salt codfish, cut in pieces · 1 cup flour · 2 1/2 cups oil for frying ·

FOR THE SAUCE:
6 tablespoons olive oil · 1 large onion, chopped · 1 garlic clove, minced · 1 tablespoon parsley, chopped · 2 tablespoons flour · 1 cup white wine · 1 cup fish stock · 1 bay leaf ·

Soak the fish overnight in enough cold water to cover. Cook the codfish in boiling water for 5 minutes; then lower heat and cook until fish is tender. Remove and dry on paper towels but reserve the fish stock. Dip each piece in flour and fry in hot fat (about 375°). Set aside in a pan.

Prepare the sauce by heating the oil in a frying pan. Cook the onion over moderate heat until it begins to brown (about 7 minutes). Crush the minced garlic and parsley together in a mortar and pestle or in a food processor. Add 2 or 3 tablespoons of the fish stock to the frying pan. Stir in the flour, crushed garlic and parsley. Blend in the wine and fish stock. More stock can be added if the mixture becomes too thick. Add the bay leaf and cook about 10 minutes. Add the fish to the sauce and cook another 10 minutes on low heat. Shake the pan from time to time to distribute the sauce evenly. Remove bay leaf. Garnish with chopped parsley. You may serve from the pan in which it was cooked.

SERVES 6-8.

Croquetas de atún

Tuna Croquettes

3 tablespoons olive oil · 3 tablespoons flour · 1/2 teaspoon salt · 1 tablespoon onion, minced · 1 cup milk · 1 tablespoon lemon juice · 2 teaspoons Worcestershire sauce · 2 cans (6 1/4 oz. size) tuna, drained and flaked · 1 1/2 cups soft bread crumbs · 2 egg yolks · 2 egg whites · 1 tablespoon olive oil · 1 cup dry bread crumbs · oil for frying ·

Heat the oil in a saucepan; blend in flour, salt, and onion. Gradually stir in milk; cook over moderate heat until thick, stirring continually. Stir in lemon juice, Worcestershire sauce, tuna, soft bread crumbs, and the egg yolks. Refrigerate for several hours. Shape into 12 patties.

Mix the egg whites with 1 tablespoon of olive oil. Dip each patty in egg white mixture; then coat with dry bread crumbs. Heat the oil to 375° (a crust of bread will brown in 1 minute). Fry in oil until the croquettes are a golden brown. Drain on paper towels and serve hot.

SERVES 6.

Variation of Croquettes

For Croquetas de salmón (Salmon Croquettes) substitute 1 1/4 cups of salmon for the tuna.

Salmón cocido

Cooked Salmon

Salmon may be cooked in CALDO CORTO (see page 107) with or without the wine. It may be cooked in the form of steaks, the entire hind section, or a whole salmon for a large group. Be sure there is enough liquid to cover the fish. Bring to a boil; then lower the heat so the salmon will cook slowly. Allow 25 min-

utes of cooking time for every 2 pounds of fish. Salmon may be served hot or cold with various sauce.

HOT: Serve with hollandaise sauce, (page 35) béchamel sauces (pages 33-34) or "Sour Cream with Dill" sauce (page 38).

COLD: Serve with all types of mayonnaises; Spanish, green, lime or tomato and cognac. Here is a chance to use the very famous ALIOLI sauce (page 30).

Rodajas de salmón al horno

Baked Salmon Steaks

6 salmon steaks ·
1 cup olive oil · salt ·
4 ounces butter ·
1 tablespoon
parsley, chopped ·
6 slices of lemon ·

Wash the steaks and drain on paper towels. Marinate the steaks in the oil for 1/2 hour on one side; then turn them and marinate for 1/2 hour on the other side.

Salt the steaks on both sides and put them in a shallow baking dish. Dot each steak with butter. Bake in preheated oven at 375° for 30 minutes until the salmon steaks flake easily when tested with a fork, and are golden brown. Periodically spoon pan juices over the fish as they cook.

Serve hot with the sauce that formed in the baking pan, garnishing each steak with parsley and serving slices of lemon on the platter.

SERVES 6.

Escabeche de pescado

Pickled Fish

3 tablespoons flour · 1 1/2 teaspoons salt · 1 1/2-2 pounds white fish fillets · 3/4 cup olive oil · 2 large onions, sliced · 1 red pepper, seeds removed and sliced · 2 garlic cloves, chopped · 1 red chili pepper, chopped · 1 bay leaf · 1/4 teaspoon whole black peppercorns · 1 1/4 cups red wine vinegar ·

Combine the flour and 1 teaspoon of the salt on a plate. Dust the fish with the flour mixture, shaking off any excess. Heat the olive oil in a heavy skillet and sauté the fish over moderate heat for 4 or 5 minutes on each side, until they are golden. Drain on paper towels. Fry the onions in the oil until they are soft. Add pepper, garlic, chili pepper, bay leaf, remaining half teaspoon of salt, peppercorns, and vinegar. Bring to boil and cook for 6 minutes.

Arrange fish in glass dish. Pour the marinade over the fish. Cover the dish. Cool to room temperature; then refrigerate for several days. May be served from the dish or removed and arranged over lettuce. For appetizers, slice in bite-size pieces and serve on toothpicks.

SERVES 4-5 OR MAY BE SERVED AS APPETIZERS SERVING 8-10.

Manera de cocer gambas

Way of Cooking Shrimp

For two pounds of fresh shrimp, bring 4 cups of water to a boil with 1 stalk of celery with the leaves, several slices of onion, and 1 1/2 teaspoons of salt. Add the shrimp. Bring to a second boil; turn off heat and let shrimp cook in the hot water for 6 to 8 minutes. The length of time will depend on the size of the shrimp, but they will be pink when they are thoroughly cooked and tender. Drain, but you may want to reserve the liquid for dishes that require fish stock. Shell the shrimp and remove the black vein. Refrigerate before serving if you plan to serve them cold with any of the following sauces.

May be served with ali-oli sauce (page 30), any of the mayonnaises (pages 31-32), Granada sauce (page 35), sour cream with dill (page 38), or the Italian-style sauce (page 41).

TWO POUNDS OF SHRIMP SERVES 6.

Gambas al ajillo

Shrimp Cooked in Garlic

2 pounds shrimp ·
1 red pepper,
chopped ·
3 or 4 garlic cloves,
finely chopped ·
1 medium onion,
chopped ·
4 tablespoons olive
oil · salt and
pepper, to taste ·

Cook shrimp according to the preceding directions listed in "Way of Cooking Shrimp." Shell and devein. Sauté the red pepper, garlic, and onion in the olive oil over medium heat. Add salt and pepper to taste. When the onion is transparent, add the shrimp and cook an additional 8-10 minutes. Serve hot.

SERVES 6.

Cocktail de gambas

Shrimp Cocktail

FOR THE SAUCE:
1 egg · juice of 1 lemon · 1 teaspoon salt · 1 cup olive oil · 1 teaspoon French's prepared mustard · 1 teaspoon tomato paste · 1 teaspoon cognac ·

3 pounds shrimp · lettuce · 1 hard-boiled egg, chopped ·

Prepare the sauce by mixing the egg, 1/2 of the lemon juice, and the salt in an electric mixer or blender at low speed. Add the oil drop by drop at first; continue to add in a thin stream until all the oil is used and the mixture is smooth and creamy. Blend in the remaining lemon juice, mustard, tomato paste, and cognac. Refrigerate for an hour or more before serving.

Prepare the shrimp according to the directions listed in "Way of Cooking Shrimp." Remove shells and devein. Refrigerate for an hour or two before serving.

Serve on lettuce leaves in shellfish cocktail glasses or bowls. Top with shrimp and then the sauce. Garnish with the hard-boiled egg and serve cold.

SERVES 6.

Gambas con gabardina

Breaded Shrimp

Remove two-thirds of the shell of the uncooked shrimp, leaving a little by the tail and the whole tail. For every 1/2 pound of shrimp, prepare a batter of 1/2 cup flour, salt to taste, and enough beer so the dough will be the consistency of a medium sauce. Holding the shrimp by the tail, dip in the batter covering all but the tail. Fry in deep fat at 375° (a crust of bread should turn brown in 1 minute) until browned. Drain on paper towels and serve hot.

May be served with any of the mayonnaises (pages 31-32), Granada sauce (page 35), sour cream with dill sauce (page 38) or Italian-style sauce (page 41).

Gambas al estilo español

Spanish-style Shrimp

4 cups bread, cut in cubes · 1/4 cup olive oil · 2 1/2 cups canned tomatoes and liquid · 1 pound shrimp, cleaned but raw · 1 tablespoon lemon juice · 1/2 cup onion, chopped · 1/4 cup parsley, chopped · 1 teaspoon salt · dash of papper ·

Sauté bread cubes in olive oil over medium heat until golden and crisp. Measure one cup of the cubes and set aside.

Combine remaining fried bread cubes with tomatoes, shrimp, lemon juice, onion, parsley, salt, and pepper.

Pour into 1 1/2 quart-baking dish. Cover and bake at 350° for 30 to 40 minutes. The mixture should be bubbly and shrimp thoroughly cooked. Sprinkle remaining bread cubes over top of casserole and cook 5 more minutes.

SERVES 4.

Almejas a la marinera

Mariner-style Clams

36 medium-sized clams · 4 tablespoons olive oil · 1 medium onion, finely chopped · 2 garlic cloves, minced · 3 medium tomatoes, peeled and chopped · 3/4 cup dry white wine · 1 bay leaf · salt and pepper, to taste · juice of 1/2 lemon · 1/4 cup parsley, minced ·

Soak the clams in water for an hour or more, changing the water several times to remove sand.

Sauté the onion and garlic in the oil over moderate heat until the onion begins to brown. Add tomatoes, wine, and bay leaf; continue to cook until sauce thickens. Add clams. Cook for several minutes until all the clams have opened. DISCARD any clams that do not open. Season with salt, pepper, and lemon juice. Remove bay leaf. Garnish with parsley and serve hot from the dish in which the clams cooked if you wish.

NOTE: It will add interest if you leave some of the clam shells in the serving dish.

SERVES 6.

Cangrejos con salsa béchamel y coñac

Crab Meat Béchamel and Cognac

FOR THE SAUCE:
3/4 cup mushrooms, cleaned and sliced · 2 tablespoons butter · 2 tablespoons olive oil · 4 tablespoons flour · 1 teaspoon salt · 1 cup milk · 1 tablespoon tomato paste · 2 tablespoons cognac · liquid from crabs · 2 egg yolks, slightly beaten ·

2 cups fresh-cooked or canned crab meat · bread crumbs · paprika ·

Sauté the mushrooms in the butter and olive oil over moderate heat for 3-5 minutes. Blend in the flour and salt. Remove from the heat. Gradually stir in the cup of milk. Pour the tomato paste, cognac, and any liquid from crab meat in another cup. Add enough water to measure one cup. Gradually stir this in the sauce. Return to heat. Stir continually until sauce is smooth. Stir some of the sauce in with the egg yolks; then add the yolks to the sauce.

In a flat casserole dish, mix the crab meat and sauce. Top with bread crumbs and paprika. Cook in hot oven at 400° about 10 minutes.

SERVES 6.

Manera de cocer la langosta

Way of Cooking Lobster

lobster meat (allow 1/2 pound per serving) · 1 medium carrot, scraped and cut in thin slices · 1 small onion, cut in two pieces · 1 bay leaf · 1/4 teaspoon thyme · sprig of parsley · 1/2 glass dry white wine · 1 tablespoon salt · 6 whole black peppers ·

In a large kettle put enough water so the lobster will be completely covered. Add the carrot, onion, bay leaf, thyme, parsley, wine, salt, and black peppers to the pot. Bring the water to a boil and plunge the lobster head first into the pot. Cover and boil from 15 to 25 minutes depending on the size of the lobster. The lobster will be bright red when it is cooked.

Manera de preparar la langosta

Way of Preparing Lobster

Follow the preceding directions for cooking the lobster. When the lobster is bright red, remove with tongs. It may be served in or removed from the shell. To remove the meat from the shell, first chop off the claws. Cut through the shell on the back of the lobster from the head to the tail. (I use kitchen scissors for this.) Discard the black vein running from head to tail and the stomach pouch that is located near the head and usually contains sand. The claws may be cracked with a nutcracker and the meat removed.

Serve with melted butter or melted butter to which a little lemon juice has been added.

Langosta a la española

Spanish-style Lobster

2 1/2 cups cooked lobster · 1/8 cup butter · 1/8 cup olive oil · 1 whole garlic clove · 2 tablespoons shallots, chopped · 1 small onion, chopped · 1/4 cup flour · 1 medium-sized tomato, peeled with seeds removed and cut in small pieces · 1 3/4 cup chicken or fish stock · 1 cup good dry white wine or Spanish sherry · all-purpose seasoning, pinch · cayenne pepper, dash · salt and pepper, to taste · 1 cup grated cheese · prasley for garnish ·

Prepare the lobster according to the preceding recipes. You may substitute 4 frozen lobster tails for the live lobster. Cook them in the same way, but reduce the cooking time to 5 minutes after the water begins to boil.

Heat the butter and the oil in a frying pan. Add garlic, shallots, and onion. Cook over low heat about 5 minutes until the onion is transparent. Discard the clove of garlic. Blend in the flour. Add the tomato pieces, allowing them to cook until soft and crushing them with the back of the spoon. Slowly add the stock, stirring continually, until the sauce thickens.

Add wine, a pinch of all-purpose seasoning, a dash of cayenne, the lobster, and salt and pepper to taste. Cook a minute or two to blend all the flavors.

Return to the lobster shells or into individual casserole dishes. Top with the grated cheese and bake at 375° for about 20 minutes or until browned. Garnish with pieces of parsley.

Good served with white rice (see page 89).

SERVES 4-6.

Mariscada a la marinera

Mariner-style Seafood

3 rock lobster tails ·
1 medium-sized
onion, chopped ·
3 garlic cloves,
crushed · 1/3 cup
olive oil · 1 pound
raw shrimp, shelled
and deveined ·
1 tablespoon lemon
juice · 1/4 cup
parsley, minced ·
powdered saffron, a
pinch ·
3/4 teaspoon salt ·
1 tablespoon soft
bread crumbs ·
1/2 cup good sherry ·
1 1/2 cups minced
clams with liquid ·

Cut lobster tails into thirds; cut away undershell. Sauté onion and garlic in olive oil until tender but not brown. Add lobster, shrimp, lemon juice, parsley, a pinch of saffron, and salt. Cover pan; cook for 3 minutes without adding any liquid.

Add bread crumbs, sherry, and clams. Cook over low heat for 5 minutes or until the shrimp are pink and the lobster meat is creamy white and the shells bright red.

Good served with rice (pages 88-90).

SERVES 6.

Caracoles a la española

Spanish-style Snails

Combine the onion, bell pepper, and ham.

1/2 cup onion, chopped · 1/2 green bell pepper, cut julienne · 1 cup raw ham, chopped · 1/4 cup olive oil · 1 garlic clove, minced · 70-75 snails (canned) · salt and pepper, to taste · 2 tablespoons parsley, chopped ·

Heat the oil in a pan until it is hot but not smoking. Add the garlic, onion, bell pepper, and ham to the oil. Cook over medium heat for about 4 minutes.

You should be able to find the snails in canned form in a fancy food or fish market. Drain the liquid from the cans. Salt and pepper the snails to taste; then add to the ham mixture.

Sauté over medium heat until the mixture begins to brown.

Serve in a deep bowl. Garnish with the parsley.

SERVES 5-6.

la carne

8

meat

Unlike the United States, when dining in an un-familiar restaurant in Spain, I would not recom-mend that you order steak. It is not that beef is really that scarce, but cows are more valuable for their milk, and the bulls of Spain are raised for bullfighting. However, I have gotten delicious filet mignon on several occasions in Burgos, Spain. I always wondered if it had come straight from the bullring and been marinating for some time. Meat from suckling animals is very popular and seems to be readily available. Not only is the veal very good, but suckling goat (kid), lamb, and pig are excellent. Ham is very popular and pieces of ham adorn many of the dishes.

Cordero a la Valencia

Valencia-style Lamb

6 lamb shanks · 1/4 cup flour · salt · 1 teaspoon pepper · 1 teaspoon paprika · 1/4 cup olive oil · 1 teaspoon rosemary, crushed ·

Coat each lamb shank with mixture of flour, salt, pepper, and paprika. Place in a shallow baking dish. Cover each piece of meat with oil and pour the rest in the baking dish. Preheat the oven to 350°. Bake un-covered for 2 1/2 to 3 hours, turning from time to time, until crisp on the outside.

For gravy, mix 1 tablespoon of the meat drippings in a pan with the flour and salt. Slowly add the water,

124

FOR THE GRAVY:
1 tablespoon flour ·
1/2 teaspoon salt ·
1 cup water ·

stirring continually over moderate heat until the gravy has thickened.

Serve with mashed potatoes or whole new potatoes.

SERVES 6.

Cordero asasdo con salsa de yemas

Roast Lamb with Egg Sauce

1 leg of lamb (3 1/2 to 4 pounds) ·
2 ounces butter ·
salt and pepper, to taste · 1 small onion · 2 sprigs parsley · 1/2 bay leaf · 1 garlic clove · 1 cup white wine · 1 cup canned tomatoes ·

Place the lamb in a shallow baking dish. Butter it and season with salt and pepper. Place two slices of onion on either side of the meat. Crush the parsley, bay leaf, and garlic clove together in a mortar and pestle or in a food processor; add them to the baking dish.

Cook in a 400° preheated oven for 10 minutes. Lower oven to 325° and add the wine. Bake for 2 hours, basting the meat from time to time. Add tomatoes and bake 30 minutes more.

FOR THE SAUCE:
2 egg yolks, beaten ·
juice of 1 lemon ·
1 1/2 tablespoons parsley, chopped ·
1 tablespoon butter ·

Slice the lamb, arranging the slices on a serving platter and keeping warm.

Pour the liquid from the baking dish into the top of a double boiler, removing all grease. Mix a little of this liquid with the egg yolks. Then add egg yolks, lemon juice, parsley, and butter to the pan. Stir continually until sauce begins to thicken. Pour over lamb, or serve in a separate dish as a gravy with boiled potatoes.

SERVES 6-8.

125

Chuletas de cordero con béchamel

Lamb Chops with Béchamel Sauce

18 small lamb chops · 1 cup olive oil · salt and pepper, to taste ·

FOR THE BÉCHAMEL: 2 tablespoons olive oil · 1 tablespoon butter · 2 1/2 tablespoons flour · salt and pepper, to taste · 2 cups cold milk ·

2 eggs, beaten · 1 plate bread crumbs ·

Season the lamb chops with salt and pepper and fry them in the oil over moderate heat for 2 or 3 minutes. Set aside.

In another frying pan over low heat, heat the butter and oil. Blend in the flour, salt, and pepper. Remove from heat; gradually stir in milk. Return to heat and stir continually until sauce is smooth.

Dip the chops in the béchamel one by one until they are well covered on both sides.

Before serving, dip the cutlets in egg and then bread crumbs. Fry in the olive oil over moderate heat until brown. Serve immediately.

SERVES 6.

Chuletas de cordero a la Navarra

Navarre-style Lamb Chops

12 medium-sized lamb chops · salt and pepper, to taste · 1/4 cup olive oil · 1 large onion, chopped · 2 garlic cloves · 1/2 cup cooked ham, chopped · 2 cups canned tomatoes, chopped · 6 ounces chorizo (or pepperoni) sausage, sliced thin ·

Season the lamb chops with salt and pepper, and fry them in the oil until they are evenly browned on both sides. Put the chops in a large shallow baking dish.

Fry the onion, garlic, and ham, in the frying pan in which the chops were fried, until the onion is soft. Stir in the tomatoes with the liquid in which they were packed. Bring to a boil, stirring occasionally.

Preheat the oven to 350°. Pour the tomato mixture over the chops and bake for 20 minutes.

Arrange the slices of sausage over mixture. Bake 20 more minutes or until the lamb chops are tender. Serve immediately.

SERVES 6.

126

Chuletas de cordero con alioli

Lamb Chops with Ali-Oli Sauce

Have your butcher cut the lamb chops about 1 inch thick, and allow 2 or 3 chops per person. Grill in the backyard over charcoal or under a broiler until brown on both sides. Cover with cold ali-oli sauce and serve immediately. (Refer to page 30 for recipe on preparing ali-oli sauce.)

Chuletas de cordero con salsa romesco

Lambs Chops with Romesco Sauce

The chops should be cut about 1 inch thick, allowing 2 or 3 chops per person. These will be better if they are grilled over charcoal, as you should baste the chops with the sauce while they are grilling. The recipe for Romesco Sauce will make 1 1/2 cups of sauce. (Refer to page 39.)

Hígado de ternera frita

Fried Calf's Liver

6 slices liver cut 1/2 inch thick · 1/2 cup of flour · 1 teaspoon salt · 1/8 teaspoon pepper · 1/2 cup oil · 1 tablespoon lemon juice · 1 whole garlic clove (optional) · 1 tablespoon parsley, chopped ·

Roll the liver in the flour that has been seasoned with salt and pepper. Fry in the oil over moderate heat until brown on both sides. Lower heat and fry for several more minutes until well done. Place on a serving platter and set aside.

Add the lemon juice and garlic (if you are using it) to the oil. Stir well for several minutes; remove garlic, and pour lemon juice mixture over liver. Garnish each piece of meat with parsley and serve immediately.

SERVES 6.

Filetes de hígado con champiñones

Liver Fillets with Mushrooms

6 slices calf's liver cut 1/2 inch thick · 1/2 cup of flour · 1 teaspoon salt · 1/8 teaspoon pepper · 1/2 cup oil ·

1/2 pound mushrooms · juice of 1/2 lemon · 2 tablespoons white wine ·

Roll the liver in the flour that has been seasoned with salt and pepper. Heat oil to 375°. (To test, place a crust of bread in the oil, which should brown in 1 minute.) Brown the meat on one side; turn over and brown on the other. Lower heat and cook slowly until the liver is well done and tender. Drain on paper towels and place on serving platter.

Clean and slice the mushrooms. Sauté the mushrooms in the oil in which the liver cooked; add more oil if necessary. Add the lemon juice and wine. Cover and cook for 5-7 minutes.

Arrange the mushrooms on top of the liver and serve immediately.

SERVES 6.

Filetes de hígado de ternera empanados

Breaded Calf's Liver

6 slices calf's liver cut 1/2 inch thick · salt and pepper, to taste · 1 garlic clove, minced · 1 sprig parsley · 1 plate fine bread crumbs · 1 or 2 eggs, beaten · 1/2 cup olive oil ·

Season the pieces of liver with salt, pepper, and the minced garlic that has been crushed with the parsley in a mortar and pestle, in a food processor, or crush with a wooden spoon. Dip each piece in bread crumbs, then egg, and again in bread crumbs. Shake off any excess.

Fry in the oil (375°) until brown on one side; turn over and brown other side. Lower heat and cook slowly until the liver is well done and tender.

SERVES 6.

Chuletas de ternera con tomate y pimientos verdes

Veal Cutlets with Tomato and Green Peppers

2 tablespoons olive oil · 6 medium-sized tomatoes, peeled and chopped · 1 tablespoon sugar · salt and pepper, to taste · 3/4 cup oil · 4 bell peppers, seeds removed and chopped · 6 veal cutlets ·

Heat the oil in a frying pan. Add the tomatoes and cook over moderate heat about 20 minutes, mashing the tomatoes with the back of a spoon frequently. Add sugar, salt, and pepper; set aside.

In another frying pan, cook the peppers in oil over very low heat. Cover and simmer for 20 minutes. Move the bell peppers to the tomato mixture with a slotted spoon and mix well. Keep warm over low heat.

Fry the cutlets, in the pan in which the bell peppers cooked, in 6 tablespoons of oil. Brown quickly on high heat; then lower heat and cook about 8 minutes on each side.

Place the cutlets on a platter and top each cutlet with the tomato-pepper mixture. Serve immediately.

SERVES 6.

Ternera a la Valenciana

Valencia-style Veal Cutlets

6 veal cutlets, pounded thin · salt and pepper, to taste · 6 thin slices ham · 1/4 cup olive oil · 1 medium-sized onion, chopped · 1 teaspoon orange rind, grated · 3/4 cup orange juice · 1/2 cup dry sherry (jerez) · 2 tablespoons flour · 2 tablespoons water ·

Season the cutlets with salt and pepper. Top each cutlet with a slice of ham. (You can buy the ham already sliced thin.) Roll so that the ham is inside and tie each roll with string or use toothpicks. Heat the oil in a frying pan, and rapidly brown each rolled cutlet. Remove to a platter using a slotted spoon.

Fry the onion until it is soft. Add orange rind and juice, and the sherry. Bring to a boil. Reduce heat to low. Return cutlet rolls to pan. Simmer for 15 to 20 minutes, turning the rolls in the sauce so they will cook evenly. Remove meat to a warm serving platter.

Mix the flour with the water until smooth (a never-fail method is to shake the flour and water together in a glass jar). Stir this mixture into the frying pan; stir continually until thick and smooth. Pour over the cutlet rolls and serve immediately.

SERVES 6.

Chuletas de ternera con higaditos de pollo

Veal Cutlets with Chicken Livers

6 veal cutlets, pounded thin · salt and pepper, to taste · 6 chicken livers · 6 sprigs of parsley · 1 medium-sized onion, peeled and thinly sliced in 6 slices · 6 teaspoons olive oil · 6 tablespoons dry white wine ·

Season the cutlets with salt and pepper. Cut each chicken liver nearly in half and place on one side of the cutlet with a sprig of parsley and the onion. Sprinkle a teaspoon of olive oil and a tablespoon of wine over each cutlet. Wrap each cutlet in aluminum foil and place in a baking dish.

Bake in a 350° preheated oven for one hour. Serve immediately.

SERVES 6.

Ternera al Jerez

Jerez-style Veal Cutlets

1/2 cup olive oil ·
1 medium onion,
chopped · 3 garlic
cloves, minced ·
1 small bell pepper,
seeds removed and
chopped · 1 cup
mushrooms, sliced ·
4 tomatoes, peeled
and chopped ·
1/2 cup cooked
ham, chopped ·
12 green olives,
seeds removed ·

6 veal cutlets,
pounded thin ·
flour · salt and
pepper · 1/2 cup
dry sherry (jerez) ·
1/4 cup water ·

Heat 1/4 cup of the olive oil in a frying pan. Fry the onion, garlic, and bell pepper until soft. Add mushrooms, tomatoes, ham, and olives; cook 20 minutes, stirring occasionally, until the mixture has thickened.

Coat the cutlets in flour that has been seasoned with salt and pepper. Heat the remaining 1/4 cup oil in a frying pan. Fry the cutlets for about 4 minutes on each side, or until they are thoroughly cooked and tender. Set aside.

Pour the sherry and water into the pan in which the cutlets cooked; bring to a boil. Add the tomato mixture from the other frying pan and mix well. Return the cutlets to the pan, covering them with the tomato mixture. Cover the pan and simmer over low heat for 5 minutes.

Serve on a platter and cover the cutlets with the sauce.

SERVES 6.

Filetes de solomillo con champiñones

Filet Mignon with Mushrooms

6 filet mignon steaks · olive oil ·

Marinate the steaks in olive oil for at least 30 minutes before cooking, turning frequently.

1 cup fresh mushrooms, cleaned and sliced · 1 tablespoon butter · juice of 1 lemon · salt, to taste ·

Cook the mushrooms with the butter, lemon juice, and salt over medium heat about 10 minutes. Set aside.

3 tablespoons oil · 2 medium onions, peeled and chopped · 1/2 cup cooked ham ·

Heat the oil in a frying pan; fry the onions over medium heat for about 5 minutes, stirring frequently. When the onion is transparent, add the ham and the mushroom mixture. Stir and keep on very low heat.

Broil the fillets over charcoal or pan fry according to individual taste (rare, medium, etc.). Serve immediately, topping each steak with some of the mushrooms, ham, and onion mixture.

SERVES 6.

Filetes de solomillo flameado con coñac

Filet Mignon Flamed with Cognac

6 filet mignon steaks · seasoned salt · whole black peppers · 3 tablespoons olive oil · 6 tablespoons good cognac ·

Sprinkle the steaks with salt, and using a pepper mill, grind fresh pepper over the steaks. Work the salt and pepper into the steaks.

Heat the oil in a heavy frying pan and sauté the steaks rapidly over high heat until browned on each side. Cooking time will vary according to the thickness of the meat, but for a 1-inch steak, allow 2 1/2 to 3 minutes on each side for rare meat.

Heat the cognac in a small pan to lukewarm. Ignite the cognac and pour flaming over the steaks.

Serve immediately.

SERVES 6.

Carne asada en marmita

Beef Pot Roast

1 small onion ·
1 garlic clove ·
1 green pepper ·
1/4 teaspoon
marjoram · 2 small
bay leaves · 1/4 cup
olive oil ·

3 to 4 pounds rump
roast of beef ·
2 cups canned
tomatoes with
liquid · 2 cups red
wine · 1/4 teaspoon
cinnamon ·
1/8 teaspoon cloves ·
2 teaspoons salt ·

Mash the onion, garlic, green pepper, marjoram, and bay leaves together with the olive oil using the back of a wooden spoon until they are the consistency of a paste. Rub into beef and let stand 1 hour.

Brown the meat in a Dutch oven or large pan. Add tomatoes, wine, cinnamon, cloves, and salt. Cover and simmer over low heat for 3 or 4 hours, or until the meat is very tender.

Serve hot, covering the meat with the sauce from the baking pan.

SERVES 6.

Platillo anticuado

Old-Fashioned Beef Stew

1 pound lean beef,
cut in cubes ·
1 tablespoon flour ·
2 tablespoons olive
oil · 4 cups tomato
juice · 1/2 cup
celery, diced ·
6 whole allspice ·
1 bay leaf ·
1/2 teaspoon salt ·
1/8 teaspoon
pepper ·
3 potatoes, peeled
and cut into cubes ·
4 carrots, scraped
and sliced ·
1 pound small
white onions,
peeled but whole ·
2 cups English
peas, fresh or
frozen ·

Coat the beef cubes with flour. Heat oil in Dutch oven or large pan; add meat and brown well.

Add 2 cups of the tomato juice, the celery, allspice, bay leaf, salt, and pepper. Bring to a boil; lower heat; cover and simmer for 1 1/2 hours.

Add remaining 2 cups tomato juice, potatoes, carrots, and onions. Simmer covered for 45 minutes more. Add peas; cook covered 20 minutes more, or until meat and vegetables are tender.

SERVES 6.

Pudín de pasta rellana de carne

Beef Stew with Dumplings

Drop the dumpling batter (page 135) by tablespoonfuls on top of the ingredients about 20 minutes before the stew is done. Cook uncovered for 10 minutes; then cover and cook 10 minutes more.

Pasta culinaria

Batter for Dumplings

1 1/2 cups sifted flour · 2 teaspoons baking powder · 1/2 teaspoon salt · 1 egg, beaten · 3/4 cup milk · 2 tablespoons olive oil ·

Mix the flour with the baking powder and salt. Beat the egg with the milk and oil. Add to the flour mixture and stir until just blended.

PASTA DE ENELDO (DILLY DUMPLINGS)   Stir 2 teaspoons dried dill weed into batter.

PASTA DE PEREJIL (PARSLEY DUMPLINGS)   Add 1/4 cup finely chopped fresh parsley to the sifted dry ingredients.

PASTA ESPECIADA (SPICY DUMPLINGS)   Add 1/4 teaspoon ground ginger and a dash of garlic powder and soy sauce to the batter.

PASTA DE QUESO (CHEESE DUMPLINGS)   Add 1/4 cup grated cheese to flour mixture before adding milk.

PASTA DE LAS SEMILLAS DE AMAPOLA (POPPY SEED DUMPLINGS)   Stir 1 teaspoon poppy seeds into batter.

Carne en ropa vieja

Meat in Old Clothes

Here is an interesting beef dish that originated in Spain called "Carne en ropa vieja" ("Meat in Old Clothes") and now is very popular in many areas of the Caribbean where it is called simply "Ropa vieja" ("Old Clothes"). In Spain the name probably originated from the fact that the cook uses leftover meat, while in this hemisphere fresh meat is boiled first and then cut into shreds.

2 1/2-3 pounds leftover beef · 4 tablespoons oil · 1 large or 2 small onions, chopped · 4 tomatoes peeled and chopped · 1 tablespoon sugar · 1/2 teaspoon salt · 1 large or 2 small green peppers · salt and pepper, to taste

Cut the leftover meat in large pieces and set aside.

Heat the oil in a frying pan. Fry the onion in the oil about 5 minutes, or until it begins to brown. Then add the tomatoes and cook for about 15 minutes, until the tomatoes are soft. Purée by placing this mixture in a blender at low speed or putting it through a colander. Add sugar and salt and set aside.

Roast the pepper in a 325° preheated oven until it is tender, about 30 minutes. Let it cook a little; then peel, remove seeds and slice in thin strips.

Put the leftover meat, tomato mixture, and green pepper in the frying pan. Season with additional salt and pepper. Simmer an additional 20 or 25 minutes.

Serve with white rice (page 89).

SERVES 6.

136

Albondigas

Meat Balls

1 pound ground
beef · 1/4 pound
ground pork ·
1/4 pound cooked
ground ham ·
1 sprig parsley,
chopped · 1 garlic
clove, finely
chopped · 2 eggs,
slightly beaten ·
1 cup fine bread
crumbs ·
3 tablespoons
white wine ·
1 teaspoon salt ·
1/2 cup olive oil ·

FOR THE SAUCE:
4 tablespoons olive
oil · 1/2 cup onion,
chopped ·
2 medium-sized
tomatoes, peeled
and chopped ·
3 cups beef
bouillon (or
3 bouillon cubes
dissolved in 3 cups
hot water) ·
1/4 teaspoon
powdered saffron ·
2 tablespoons
flour ·

Mix the ground beef, pork, and ham together; set aside. In a large bowl, mix the parsley, garlic, eggs, bread crumbs, wine, and salt; then thoroughly mix in the meats. Form into balls about 1 inch or more in diameter.

Heat the oil in a frying pan. Fry the meat balls in the oil, turning them frequently so they will brown evenly. When they are brown, put them in a large pan so they will not be crowded and prepare the sauce.

Heat the oil in a frying pan and fry the onion about 5 minutes or until it begins to brown. Add the tomatoes and cook another 6 to 8 minutes, crushing the tomatoes with the back of a spoon as they cook. When the tomatoes are soft, add the bouillon and saffron. Bring to a boil. Purée by placing this mixture in a blender at low speed or putting it through a colander. Return to the frying pan over low heat. Stir in the flour, which should be mixed with a little water first to keep it smooth. Continue to stir until the sauce is well mixed.

Pour the sauce over the meat balls and simmer for one hour.

SERVES 6.

Filetes picados en salsa con cebolla

Hamburgers in Sauce with Onion

1 1/2 pounds ground lean beef · salt · 1/2 cup flour · 1/4 cup oil · 1 large onion, peeled and sliced · 1 cup white wine · 1/2 cup water ·

Divide the ground meat into 6 portions. Shape into balls; then flatten out into patties 1/2 inch thick. Season with salt on both sides and coat with flour.

Heat the oil, and fry the hamburgers over moderate heat, browning them on both sides. Move the hamburgers to a pan large enough so none will be stacked on top of another.

Leave at least 3 tablespoons of oil in the frying pan. Fry the onion over moderate heat until it begins to brown. Blend in 1 tablespoon flour. Slowly add the wine and water, stirring constantly for 5 minutes. Pour the sauce over the hamburgers and bake in a 325° preheated oven for 15 minutes.

Serve on a platter with the sauce.

SERVES 6.

Rollo de carne picada asada

Meat Loaf

1 egg, beaten ·
1/2 cup milk ·
3/4 cup bread
crumbs · 1 sprig
parsley, chopped ·
1 garlic clove,
crushed ·
2 tablespoons
onion, finely
chopped (or
substitute prepared
onion flakes) ·
1 1/2 pounds
ground beef ·
3 tablespoons
white wine · 1 1/2
teaspoons salt ·
1/4 teaspoon
pepper ·

Combine egg and milk; soak bread crumbs in milk mixture for 10 minutes.

In a large bowl mix together the parsley, garlic, onion, meat, soaked bread crumbs, wine, salt, and pepper. Shape into a loaf in a shallow glass baking dish.

Bake in a 350° preheated oven for 45 minutes to 1 hour, basting the meat as it cooks.

May be served hot or cold.

SERVES 6.

Chuletas de cerdo a la Aragón

Aragonese-style Pork Chops

1 garlic clove, crushed ·
1 teaspoon paprika ·
pinch of powdered cloves · 1/4 cup olive oil ·

6 lean pork chops ·
2 tablespoons flour ·
1 teaspoon salt ·
2 tablespoons olive oil · 1/2 cup onion, chopped ·
1 tomato, peeled and chopped ·
2 tablespoons vinegar · 1 cup chicken broth ·
pinch of powdered saffron ·

Combine garlic, paprika, cloves, and olive oil. Rub into chops, let stand for several hours or overnight in the refrigerator. Drain; coat with flour to which the salt has been added. Heat 2 tablespoons of oil in a frying pan. Quickly brown the chops; then remove and set them aside.

Add onion to the frying pan; cook over moderate heat until tender. Add tomato, vinegar, broth, and saffron. Bring to a boil, mashing the tomatoes with the back of a spoon. Reduce heat; return chops to sauce. Mix some of the sauce over chops; cover and simmer for about 25 minutes or until the meat is tender.

SERVES 6.

Chuletas de cerdo con cebollas en salsa

Pork Chops with Onion in Sauce

6 lean pork chops ·
salt and pepper ·
4 tablespoons oil ·
3 medium-sized onions, peeled and chopped ·

FOR THE SAUCE:
1 tablespoon butter ·
1 tablespoon olive oil · 2 tablespoons flour · 1 cup cold milk ·

Salt and pepper the chops a couple of hours before cooking them.

Heat the oil in a frying pan and fry the chops over medium heat 10 minutes on one side; turn and fry 10 minutes on the other side. Set aside, but keep warm.

Leave 3 tablespoons of oil in the frying pan. Fry the onions for several minutes; then add just enough hot water to cover them. Cook over low heat for 15 minutes.

While the onion is cooking, melt the butter with the olive oil in another frying pan over low heat. Blend in

the flour. Remove from the heat and gradually stir in the milk. Return to the heat and stir constantly for about 5 minutes. Add the onions and their juice; cook another 5 minutes or until the sauce begins to thicken.

Place the pork chops on a platter. Cover them with the onion sauce and serve immediately.

SERVES 6.

Chuletas de cerdo con salsa de tomate

Pork Chops with Tomato Sauce

6 lean pork chops ·
salt and pepper ·
4 tablespoons oil ·
1 medium onion,
peeled and chopped ·
6 medium-sized
tomatoes, peeled
and chopped ·
1 garlic clove,
crushed · 1 bay leaf ·
thyme, a pinch ·
1/2 teaspoon salt ·
1/2 cup white wine ·

Salt and pepper the pork chops a couple of hours before frying.

Heat 2 tablespoons of the oil in a frying pan; fry the onion over moderate heat—about 5 minutes, or until it is transparent. Add the tomatoes, garlic, bay leaf, thyme, salt, and wine. Bring to a boil; lower heat and simmer 3 minutes, stirring frequently. Purée by mixing in a blender at low speed or putting the mixture through a colander. Return to the frying pan and simmer until the sauce begins to thicken.

In another frying pan, heat the remaining 2 tablespoons of oil. Fry the pork chops over moderate heat about 8 minutes on each side, turning only once. They should be well-done. Place them on a platter, and serve covering each chop with tomato sauce.

SERVES 6.

Chuletas de cerdo con cerveza y cebolla

Pork Chops with Beer and Onion

6 lean pork chops ·
salt and pepper ·
4 tablespoons oil ·
2 large onions,
peeled and cut in
thin round slices ·
beer ·

Salt and pepper the pork chops on both sides a couple of hours before cooking.

Heat the oil. Quickly brown the chops; remove from pan and set aside. Put half the onion rings in the oil in which the meat fried. Place the meat on top and cover the meat with the other half of the onions. Cover the pan and cook over low heat for about 10 minutes. The onions should be transparent. Add enough beer to cover the chops. Cover the pan again and cook over low heat for 2 to 2 1/2 hours, or until the meat is well-done. Check from time to time to make sure the meat is not sticking.

Serve on a platter with the sauce from the baking pan and the onions on top of the meat.

SERVES 6.

Cerdo asado con piña

Roast Pork with Pineapple

3 1/2 to 4 pounds
pork roast · salt ·
3 tablespoons
prepared mustard ·
1 tablespoon
shortening ·
6 whole slices of
canned pineapple in
syrup ·
1 tablespoon
cornstarch ·

Salt the meat and cover it with mustard a couple of hours before cooking.

Melt the shortening in a roasting pan, and brown the meat on all sides. Bake in a 350° preheated oven for 2 1/2 hours or more, allowing at least 40 minutes per pound of meat. Pork should always be cooked well-done. Water may have to be added to the pan periodically.

When the roast is well-done, slice and place on serving platter. Cover with foil to keep warm.

Drain the pineapple slices, reserving their syrup. Dip

each slice in the liquid in the roasting pan. Slice in half, placing the slices on top and around the pork slices.

Measure the liquid in the roasting pan. Add enough pineapple syrup and water (if necessary) to measure 1 3/4 cups. Dissolve the cornstarch in a little water. Blend the cornstarch in the roasting pan with its liquid and the pineapple mixture. Stir constantly until the mixture is smooth. Serve the sauce in a separate dish.

SERVES 6.

Lomo de cerdo con manzanas

Pork Loin with Apples

3 1/2 to 4 pounds pork loin roast · salt · 2 tablespoons Crisco or other shortening · 6 small baking apples · 6 teaspoons brown sugar · 6 teaspoons dry sherry · 1 tablespoon cornstarch ·

Salt the meat a couple of hours before cooking.

Melt the shortening in the roasting pan. Add the meat and bake at 350° for 2 1/2 or 3 hours, allowing at least 40 minutes per pound of meat. Turn the roast several times during cooking so it will brown evenly. Also, add a small amount of water periodically.

Half an hour before the roast is done, cut the apples in half. Remove the core and seeds. Place 1/2 teaspoon of sugar in the core of each apple half. Put the apples around the roast and sprinkle them with sherry, about 1/2 teaspoon on each half.

When the roast is well-done, slice and place on serving platter, surrounded with the apples.

Dissolve the cornstarch in a little water and mix with the meat drippings. Stir constantly until the gravy is smooth, adding more water if necessary. Pour over the meat and serve immediately.

SERVES 6.

Jamón con espinacas y salsa de Madeira

Ham with Spinach and Madeira Sauce

**2 pounds fresh spinach or 2 packages frozen ·
1 teaspoon salt ·**

SAUCE FOR SPINACH:
**1 tablespoon butter ·
1 tablespoon olive oil ·
1 1/2 tablespoons flour · 1/2 teaspoon salt · 1 cup cold milk ·**

6 ham slices ·

SAUCE FOR HAM:
**3 tablespoons oil ·
1 small onion, peeled and chopped ·
1 tablespoon flour ·
1/2 cup water ·
1 bouillon cube (beef, chicken, etc.) ·
1/2 cup Madeira wine, or substitute sherry · butter ·**

For fresh spinach, discard the roots and tough stems. Wash the spinach carefully under running water. Cook in a heavy pan, slowly at first, without adding water. Add 1 teaspoon of salt; cover, and cook over moderate heat from 7 to 10 minutes. Stir several times. Drain and chop; keep hot while preparing the sauce. Frozen spinach should be prepared following the instructions on the package.

For the sauce, melt the butter with the oil over low heat. Blend in the flour and salt. Remove from heat and gradually stir in milk. Return to heat and cook, stirring constantly, until the sauce is thick. Set aside, but keep warm.

While preparing the sauce for the ham, fry the ham slowly in a frying pan, to which a little oil has been added.

For the ham sauce, heat the oil in a frying pan; fry the onion over moderate heat about 7 minutes, or until it begins to brown. Blend in the flour. Slowly add the water, in which the bouillon cube has been melted, and the wine. Cook over low heat about 10 minutes. Add a little butter before serving.

Serve on a platter, with the spinach covered with its sauce on one half and the ham and its sauce on the other; or you may prefer to arrange the ham slices in the middle, with the spinach on either side.

SERVES 6.

144

las aves y la caza

9

poultry and game

Among the domesticated fowl in Spain, chicken is by far the most popular. One can even purchase chicken as TAPAS, an appetizer served in the late afternoon. As chickens in the United States are usually bigger and more tender, these chicken dishes should be better than the Spanish originals. Although turkey will be found on the menu under AVES (birds), the second most popular domesticated fowl is duck. These are delicious and tender. Many varieties of wild birds also find their way to the Spanish kitchens, like partridge, (which you can even buy canned) pheasant, quail, and pigeon.

We know that man hunted on the Iberian Peninsula in the late Paleolithic culture (35,000 BC) as depicted in the "repustrian art" in the Cave of Altimira in the north and the hunting scenes in the Cave of Alpera in the southeastern part of the country. Early man believed that if he drew pictures of food animals, he could assure their multiplication and his mastery over them in hunting. On the walls of caves he painted horses, deer, goats, bison, reindeer, the wooly rhinoceros and other animals.

Even the name SPAIN goes back to wild game. It was attributed to the Phoenicians, a Semitic race, who were a seacoast people concentrating on trade and colonization. They settled in Gadir (present

146

day Cádiz) around 1100 BC. Here, as in all the Peninsula, rabbits were in abundance, but were unknown to them. Thus, SPAIN was derived from the Phoenician I-SAPHAN-IM, meaning coast or island of the rabbits.

Higaditos de pollo

Chicken Livers

about 40 chicken livers · 4 tablespoons oil · 2 large onions, peeled and chopped · salt and pepper, to taste · 1 cup white wine ·

Heat the oil in a frying pan. Fry the onions over medium heat about 5 minutes. Then add the chicken livers, salt, and pepper. Cook over low heat about 10 minutes, turning the livers frequently. Add the wine; cover the pan, and cook slowly at least 15 minutes more.

SERVES 6.

Pollo a la Chilindrón

Chilindrón-style Chicken

Here is a chicken dish popular in Aragón and Navarra.

3 1/2 to 4 pounds small chicken pieces · 3 tablespoons olive oil · 2 garlic cloves · 4 ounces ham, diced · 1 large onion, chopped · 1 small jar pimientos, drained and chopped · 1 cup canned tomatoes and juice · 1/2 cup chicken broth · marjoram, pinch · thyme, pinch · salt and pepper, to taste ·

Heat the oil in a frying pan, and fry the chicken with the whole garlic over moderate heat until golden brown. Remove chicken and set aside. Brown the ham in the oil and set aside with the chicken. Cook onion and pimientos in the oil until the onion is soft. Add the tomatoes, chicken broth, marjoram, thyme, salt, and pepper. Simmer several minutes.

Return the chicken and ham to the pan, and simmer an additional 20-25 minutes.

Remove garlic cloves before serving.

SERVES 5-6.

Pollo con salsa de champiñones

Chicken with Mushroom Sauce

5 1/2 pounds of chicken pieces · 4 tablespoons oil · 1 small onion, finely chopped · 1 can (10 3/4 ozs.) cream of mushroom soup · 1/2 cup white wine · 1 garlic clove, crushed · 1 bay leaf · thyme, a pinch · 1 sprig parsley, chopped · salt and pepper, to taste · 1/2 pound fresh mushrooms · 3 tablespoons butter · juice of 1/2 lemon · salt, a pinch ·

Heat the oil in a frying pan, and fry the chicken over moderate heat until golden brown. Set aside. Fry the onion in the same oil, stirring frequently about 5 minutes, or until it begins to brown. Return the chicken to the pan. Mix the mushroom soup with the wine. Add this to the pan along with the garlic, bay leaf, thyme, parsley, and a little salt and pepper to taste. Cover and cook over moderate heat from 45 minutes to an hour depending on the size of the chicken pieces.

Clean and chop the mushrooms. Sauté the mushrooms in the butter with the lemon juice and salt for about 10 minutes.

When the chicken is tender, remove the bay leaf, add the mushroom mixture, stir and serve.

SERVES 6-8.

Pollo guisado con cerveza y cebollas

Chicken Cooked with Beer and Onions

3 1/2 to 4 pound chicken · salt · 1/4 cup oil · 3 medium-sized onions, peeled and sliced in rings · 1 1/2 cups beer ·

Salt the cavity of the chicken. Heat the oil in a Dutch oven or large pan, and brown the chicken on all sides. Set chicken aside. Pour out any excess oil, but leave enough to cover the bottom of the pan.

Fry the onions in the oil about 6 minutes or until they are transparent. Return the chicken to the pan. Add the beer and a little more salt. Bring to a boil. Cover and cook on very low heat for about 1 1/2 hours, or until the chicken is tender. Turn the chicken several times while cooking and spoon the sauce over it.

When tender, slice the chicken and arrange on a plat-

149

ter. Strain the sauce through a colander. Arrange the onion rings around the chicken and serve.

SERVES 6.

Suprema de pollo

Chicken Supreme

4 chicken breasts ·
1 large onion,
peeled and sliced in
fourths · 2 large
carrots, scraped
and sliced ·
1 chicken bouillon
cube · salt, a pinch

FOR THE SUPREME
SAUCE:
2 tablespoons
butter ·
2 tablespoons flour ·
1 1/2 cups chicken
broth · 2 egg yolks ·
salt, to taste ·

Place the chicken breasts in a pan with enough water to cover with the onion, carrot slices, bouillon cube, and salt. Bring to a boil; lower heat and cook 1/2 an hour or more. The chicken should be very tender. Remove from the pan, but reserve the broth. Remove skin; debone; slice, and arrange on a platter.

Prepare the sauce by melting the butter in a pan over low heat. Blend in the flour; gradually stir in 1 1/2 cups of the broth in which the chicken cooked, which should be warm but not hot. Beat the egg yolks in a cup with a little salt. Add a little sauce to the yolks; then blend them into the sauce. Cover the chicken with the sauce and refrigerate.

This dish is served cold and is popular for a cold late supper, but it may be served hot.

SERVES 4.

Pollo relleno

Stuffed Chicken

1/2 cup olive oil ·
3/4 cup celery,
chopped · 1/2 cup
onion, chopped ·
4 cups dry bread
cubes ·

For the stuffing, heat oil in large frying pan; sauté celery and onion until tender, but not browned. Add bread crumbs, thyme, marjoram, sage, salt, and pepper. Heat until browned lightly and oil is absorbed. Set aside to cool.

150

1/2 teaspoon thyme ·
1/2 teaspoon
marjoram ·
1/2 teaspoon sage ·
1 teaspoon salt ·
1/8 teaspoon
pepper ·
4 to 5 pound
roasting hen · salt ·
parsley · 2 oranges,
sliced ·

Salt the neck and body cavity of the hen. Fill the neck opening 3/4 full of the stuffing; lap the skin over onto back and fasten with skewer or toothpick. Fill the body cavity 3/4 full of the stuffing and tie legs together.

Roast chicken breast side up in shallow baking dish in a 350° preheated oven 2 1/2 to 3 hours. To be sure the chicken is done, pierce with a two pronged fork in the thickest part of the breast. The juice that comes out should show no sign of red.

Put the chicken on a serving platter surrounded by the stuffing. Garnish the hen with a little parsley and place orange slices in between helpings of stuffing.

SERVES 6.

Pollo a la Catalana

Catalan-style Chicken

3 1/2 to 4 pounds
chicken pieces ·
1 ounce butter ·
3 tablespoons olive
oil · 6 small
onions, peeled and
chopped ·
1 tablespoon flour ·
1 cup chicken broth ·
1 cup white wine ·
2 tablespoons
tomato purée ·
1/8 teaspoon
ground cumin ·
1 teaspoon salt ·
1/8 teaspoon
pepper ·

Heat the butter and oil in a frying pan and fry the chicken pieces over moderate heat until golden but not brown. Place the chicken in a casserole dish. Fry the onions in the frying pan in which the chicken fried until they begin to brown, and put them over the chicken in the casserole dish. Remove all but 1 tablespoon of fat from the frying pan. Shake the flour and chicken broth together in a jar; then, slowly add to the frying pan, stirring constantly. Blend in the wine, tomato purée, cumin, salt, and pepper.

Bake in a 350° preheated oven covered for 1 hour, or until the chicken is tender.

SERVES 5-6.

151

Pollo a la española

Spanish-style Chicken

chicken, cut in 8 serving pieces or 4 breasts · 1/4 cup olive oil · 1 garlic clove, crushed · 2 medium onions, chopped · 1 large red pepper, seeds removed and chopped · 1 1/2 cups canned artichoke hearts, drained · 2 cups chicken broth · 1/4 teaspoon cayenne pepper · 1/4 teaspoon powdered saffron · 1/2 teaspoon salt · 1/8 teaspoon black pepper · 1 teaspoon butter · 1 1/2 tablespoons flour · 12 stuffed green olives, cut in halves ·

Heat the oil in a frying pan, and fry the chicken over medium heat until golden brown. Place the chicken in a casserole dish.

Fry the garlic, onion, and red pepper in the oil until they are soft. Add the artichoke hearts and fry about 3 minutes. Stir in the chicken broth, cayenne pepper, saffron, salt, and black pepper. Bring to a boil, stirring frequently. Pour the broth mixture over the chicken.

Bake in a 350° preheated oven covered for 1 hour, or until the chicken is tender. Transfer the chicken pieces to a serving platter but keep warm.

Melt the butter and blend in the flour over medium heat. Gradually stir the flour mixture into the broth mixture, stirring continually until the sauce begins to thicken and is smooth. Blend in the olives; pour sauce over chicken and serve immediately.

SERVES 4.

Pollo con arroz

Chicken with Rice

3 to 3 1/2 pounds chicken pieces · 1/2 pound lean ham, cut in pieces · 1/4 cup olive oil · 2 small onions, peeled and chopped · 1 garlic clove, crushed · 1 cup uncooked rice · 2 small tomatoes, peeled and chopped · 1 small jar pimientos, drained and chopped · 1 bay leaf · 1/8 teaspoon ground saffron · 2 cups chicken broth · 1/2 cup white wine · salt, to taste ·

Fry the chicken and ham in the oil over medium heat until well browned. Remove to a casserole dish and keep warm.

Fry the onion and garlic in the oil until they begin to brown. Add rice and cook a couple of minutes more; then add tomatoes, pimientos, bay leaf, saffron, chicken broth, wine, and salt to taste. Bring to a boil; reduce heat and cook 10 minutes, stirring frequently.

Pour this mixture over the chicken and ham in the casserole. Bake in a 325° preheated oven for about 45 minutes. Remove bay leaf and serve hot.

SERVES 4-5.

153

Empanada Gallega

Galician-style Chicken Pie

Try this version of the very famous EMPANADA that originated in Galicia. Although EMPANADA may be a hot or cold dish, this one is served hot.

FOR THE PASTRY:
4 cups flour ·
3/4 teaspoon baking powder ·
1 teaspoon salt ·
1/4 teaspoon ground cloves ·
1/2 cup olive oil ·
3/4 cup water ·

To make the pastry, sift the flour, baking powder, salt, and cloves together in a large bowl. Make a hole in the center, and pour in the oil and water. Blend the liquid with the flour with your hands or a large spoon until the dough does not stick to the sides of the bowl. Knead the dough on a lightly floured surface until smooth. Place in a bowl in a warm place covered with a damp cloth.

FOR THE FILLING:
1-3 1/2 to 4 pound chicken, cut in serving pieces ·
1 medium-sized onion, quartered ·
1/2 teaspoon whole peppercorns ·
1 teaspoon salt ·
1/4 cup olive oil ·
2 garlic cloves, crushed · 1 small onion, chopped ·
1 green pepper, seeds removed and chopped · 1/2 cup ham, chopped ·
4 medium-sized tomatoes, peeled and chopped ·

1 egg white ·
2 teaspoons milk ·

Put the chicken in a large pan with enough water to cover. Add onion, peppercorns, and salt. Bring to a boil, reduce heat, and simmer covered for 1 hour or until the chicken is tender. Remove the pieces of chicken with tongs and set aside to cool. When cool, remove skin, debone and cut in bite size pieces.

Heat the oil in a large frying pan. Fry the garlic, onion, and green pepper until soft. Then stir in ham, tomatoes and chicken pieces. Cook about 10 more minutes, stirring constantly until the tomatoes are soft.

Divide dough in two and roll each part on lightly floured surface. Carefully put 1 part of dough into a greased baking dish. Add the filling, leaving a 1/2- to 1-inch margin around the edges of the dough. Carefully arrange the second piece over the filling. Press the edges together to seal them. Cut a deep slit for air in the center of the dough. Beat the egg white with the 2 teaspoons of milk, and brush top of pastry with this mixture.

Bake in a 375° preheated oven for 30 to 40 minutes or until the crust is golden brown. Serve immediately.

SERVES 6.

154

Pavo asado

Roast Turkey

8-10 pound turkey ·
6-8 tablespoons
cognac · Crisco or
other vegetable
shortening ·
6 bacon slices ·
juice of 1 lemon ·
2 cups hot water ·
1 teaspoon salt ·

A couple of days before roasting the turkey, pour the cognac in the cavity. Move the turkey around periodically to marinate the inside evenly. Before roasting, remove any cognac that remains.

Place the turkey breast side up in a large roasting pan. Brush the skin lightly with shortening. Put 5 bacon slices over the breast and the remaining one in the cavity. Cover the breast with foil. Roast in a preheated 350° oven, allowing 20-25 minutes per pound of bird. Baste frequently. During the last half hour of roasting, remove the foil so the turkey will brown.

Place the turkey on a serving platter. For easier carving, let the turkey stand for 20 to 30 minutes. Remove any excess grease from the roasting pan. Add the lemon juice, hot water, and salt. Scrape the bottom of the pan to get all the drippings, and serve the sauce in a bowl.

SERVES 12-14.

Pavo relleno

Stuffed Turkey

8-10 pound turkey ·
salt ·

FOR THE STUFFING:
2 tablespoons
shortening · turkey
liver, chopped ·
1/2 pound ham,
chopped ·
1/2 pound pork link
sausages, sliced ·
2 slices bacon ·
1 cup prunes, seeds
removed · 1 pound
chestnuts
(optional) · 1/2 cup
mushrooms, sliced ·
thyme, a pinch ·
marjoram, a pinch ·
1 teaspoon parsley ·
1 teaspoon salt ·
black pepper, a few
grains · 1 egg,
beaten · 3/4 cup dry
sherry · Crisco or
other vegetable
shortening ·

Salt the neck and body cavity of the turkey.

Prepare the stuffing by melting the shortening and browning the turkey liver and ham. Add the sausages, bacon, prunes, chestnuts (if you are adding chestnuts, they should be shelled, boiled, and chopped), mushrooms, thyme, marjoram, parsley, salt, and pepper. Continue to cook another 15 minutes over medium heat. Remove from the heat; chop the ingredients fairly fine. Mix in the egg and sherry.

Fill the neck opening nearly full; lap the skin over onto back and fasten with skewer or toothpick. Fill the body cavity nearly full and tie legs together.

Place the turkey breast side up in a roasting pan. Brush the skin lightly with shortening. Cover the breast with foil. Roast in a preheated 350° oven, allowing 20-25 minutes per pound of bird and an additional 30-40 minutes because the turkey is stuffed. Baste frequently. During the last half hour of roasting, remove foil so the turkey will brown.

Place the turkey on a serving platter and the stuffing in a bowl.

SERVES 12-14.

Pato braseado con aceitunas

Braised Duck with Olives

6 pound duck, or
2-3 to 3 1/2 pound
ducks · salt and
pepper · flour ·
1/4 cup olive oil ·
1 large onion,
sliced · 2 large
carrots, scraped
and sliced · 2 large
tomatoes, peeled
and chopped ·
1/4 cup white wine ·
1 cup chicken
broth ·
1 1/2 teaspoons
cornstarch ·
12 pimiento-stuffed
olives, sliced ·

Cut the duck in serving pieces. Wash under running water and wipe dry. Sprinkle with salt and pepper. Dust each piece in flour.

Heat the olive oil in a frying pan and brown the pieces of duck. Use tongs for turning the pieces. While the duck is browning, add onions and carrots. Cook slowly about 15 minutes. Drain off fat, if necessary.

Add the tomatoes and cook another 10 minutes. Then add the wine and broth. Cover the pan and cook slowly 1 hour.

Remove the pieces of duck from liquid. Purée the tomato sauce in a blender or food processor. Return to the pan. Blend the cornstarch in a little water and stir into the tomato mixture. Add olives and duck pieces. Cook over low heat another 10 or 15 minutes. Serve on a platter covering the pieces of duck with the sauce.

SERVES 6.

Pato a la naranja

Orange-style Duck

6 pound duck, or 2-3 to 3 1/2 pound ducks and duck giblets · 2 cups cold water · salt ·

3 medium or 4 small oranges · 2 tablespoons shortening · 1 large carrots, scraped and sliced · 2 or 3 small onions, peeled and sliced · 1 cup white wine · 1 cup duck broth ·

1 tablespoon cornstarch · 2 tablespoons Curaçao (optional) · salt, to taste ·

Put the duck giblets in a pan with 2 cups of cold water and a little salt. Bring to a boil; lower heat to medium and cook 30 minutes. Remove and strain broth.

Peel and slice 1 or 2 of the oranges depending on the number of ducks. Fill the cavity with orange slices.

Melt the shortening in a frying pan and brown the duck(s). While the duck is browning, add the carrot and onions. Turn the duck so that it browns on all sides. Add wine, 1 cup of the broth in which the giblets cooked, and the juice of 1/2 an orange (more if the oranges are small). Cover the pan and cook over medium heat for 1 hour. Remove duck; discard the oranges from cavity.

Dissolve the cornstarch in a little water. Remove the grease from the sauce. To the sauce add cornstarch, the juice from the remaining oranges, Curaçao, a liqueur with a sour orange flavor (optional), salt to taste, and a piece of orange peel—cut in slivers with no white membrane. Blend the sauce together for several minutes.

Slice the duck according to the following drawing. Serve on a platter garnished with orange slices and the sauce as a side dish.

Good served with potatoes or rice and a green vegetable.

SERVES 6.

TO CARVE DUCK

158

Perdices con setas

Partridges with Mushrooms

4 young partridges (1 pound each) or 2 rock Cornish hens (about 2 pounds each) · salt · 2 pieces white bread, crusts removed · 3/4 cup hot milk · 2 tablespoons olive oil · 1 pound mushrooms, cleaned and chopped · livers from the birds · 1 small onion, peeled and chopped · 1 tablespoon parsley, chopped · 5 tablespoons vegetable oil · 1/4 cup cognac · 3/4 cup warm water · salt and pepper · thyme, a pinch · bay leaf, a pinch · parsley, a pinch · 1 garlic clove, crushed ·

Salt the cavities of the birds. Soak the bread in the hot milk.

Heat the oil in a frying pan over moderate heat. Add 1/2 cup of the mushrooms and the partridge or Cornish hen livers. Cook about 5 minutes; then crush the livers with a fork and add the soaked bread, onion, and parsley. Mix and cook over moderate heat for several more minutes and chop the bread as it fries. Stuff the cavities of the birds with the bread mixture, sewing the cavities or tying the legs of the bird to hold the stuffing in place.

Warm the oil in a baking pan. Add the birds. Heat the cognac in a small pan to lukewarm. Set aflame and pour flaming over the birds. Arrange the remaining mushrooms in the pan around the birds; add the water and salt and pepper the birds. Add thyme, bay leaf, parsley, and garlic.

Bake covered in a 350° oven for 30 minutes; remove cover; raise heat to 400° for 15 minutes to brown the birds.

To serve: Cut the birds in half lengthwise; put the stuffing and the mushrooms on the platter with the birds and serve immediately.

SERVES 4.

Perdices escabechadas

Pickled Partridges

4 young partridges
(1 pound each) or
2 rock Cornish
hens (about
2 pounds each) ·
1/4 cup olive oil ·
1 medium-sized
onion, peeled and
chopped ·
3 medium carrots,
scraped and sliced ·
thyme, a pinch ·
2 small bay leaves ·
1 sprig parsley,
chopped · 1 stalk
celery, chopped ·
2 garlic cloves,
crushed · 6 whole
black peppers ·
3/4 cup white wine ·
2 tablespoons
vinegar · salt, to
taste ·

Fry the birds in the oil over moderate heat until brown and place them on a plate. Leave just enough oil to cover the bottom of the pan. Fry the onion, carrots, thyme, bay leaves, parsley, celery, garlic, and peppers together over low heat. Return the partridges to the pan, and cook for 5 minutes. Add wine and vinegar. Cover pan and cook over moderate heat for 10 minutes. Add salt to taste; add enough water to barely cover the birds. Cook on low heat 1 hour or more until the birds are very tender. Let the partridges cool in their sauce.

To serve: Divide each bird into 2 serving pieces. Place on a serving platter with the carrots. Purée the sauce in a blender or food processor and pour over the birds. This dish is served cold.

SERVES 4.

160

Perdices estofadas

Stewed Partridges

4 young partridges
(about 1 pound
each) or 2 rock
Cornish hens
(about 2 pounds
each) · salt ·
1/3 cup oil ·
1 small onion,
peeled and chopped ·
2 small tomatoes,
peeled and chopped ·
1/2 cup white
wine ·
2 tablespoons
vinegar · thyme, a
pinch · 1 bay leaf ·
1 garlic clove,
crushed · 2 sprigs
parsley, chopped ·
1/2 teaspoon salt ·
1 cup water ·
4 carrots, scraped
and sliced · 8 small
whole onions,
peeled ·

Salt the cavity of the birds. Heat the oil in a large frying pan; and brown the partridges over moderate heat. Remove to a plate. Fry the onion in the oil; return the birds to the pan, and sauté them a few more minutes. Add the tomatoes, wine, vinegar, thyme, bay leaf, garlic, parsley, and salt. Cook over low heat about 15 minutes. Add water and cook on low heat an hour or more until the birds are very tender. Add more water if necessary.

In a separate pan, cook the carrots and onions in just enough water to cover for about 20 minutes. Add them to the pan in which the birds are cooking.

To serve: Divide each bird into 2 serving pieces. Place on a platter with the carrots and whole onions. Purée the sauce in a blender or food processor and pour over the birds. Serve hot.

SERVES 4.

Faisán

Pheasant

1-4 to 4 1/2 pound pheasant · salt · 4 slices bacon, sliced thin · vegetable shortening · 1 1/2 cups canned chicken broth · 1/4 pound ham, cut in cubes · 2 medium carrots, scraped and sliced · 1 tablespoon seasoned bread crumbs · 1 small can English peas · parsley sprigs ·

Salt the cavity of the bird. Tie the bacon slices around the bird. Brush the bird with vegetable shortening, and roast in a 300° oven for about 45 minutes, turning from time to time to cook evenly on all sides.

Remove the bacon; slice the pheasant in serving pieces. Put the pieces in a pan along with any drippings from the roasting pan, the chicken broth, ham, carrots, and bread crumbs. Cook over moderate heat about 30 minutes, or until the carrots and pheasant are tender. Add the canned peas and cook another 5 or 10 minutes. Serve on a platter garnished with sprigs of parsley.

SERVES 4.

Pichones guisados con aceitunas

Stewed Squabs with Olives

4 squabs · salt and pepper · flour · 1/4 cup olive oil · 1 large onion, sliced · 2 large carrots, scraped and sliced · 2 large tomatoes, peeled and chopped · 1/4 cup white wine · 1 cup canned chicken broth · 1 tablespoon cornstarch, scant · 12 pimiento-stuffed olives, sliced ·

Cut the squabs into two serving pieces each. Wash under running water and wipe dry. Sprinkle with salt and pepper. Dust each piece with flour.

Heat the oil in a frying pan and brown the pieces of squab. Use tongs for turning the pieces. While the birds are browning, add onion and carrots. Cook over low heat about 15 minutes. Add tomatoes and cook 5 or 10 minutes, mashing them with the back of a spoon as they cook. Then add wine and broth. Cover the pan and cook slowly for 30 minutes. The squabs should be tender.

Set the birds aside. Purée the sauce in which they cooked in a blender or food processor. Return to the pan. Mix the cornstarch in a little water and stir into

162

the tomato mixture. Add olives and squabs. Cook over low heat another 10 minutes. Serve on a platter covering the birds with the sauce.

SERVES 4.

Codornices en pimientos

Quail in Peppers

12 quail · salt · 12 bacon strips, thin sliced · 12 large bell peppers · 5 tablespoons oil ·

Salt the quail inside and out. Wrap each bird in bacon. Remove the stem and seeds from the pepper. Put a quail in each pepper.

Heat the oil in a large frying pan. Cook the peppers over low heat, covered. From time to time, turn the peppers carefully using tongs. Cook about 45 minutes and serve hot with the juice from the pan.

SERVES 6.

Remember that the name SPAIN was derived from a Phoenician expression, meaning coast or island of the rabbits. Today rabbit is still a popular dish in Spain. The Spanish cooks prefer the wild rabbits to the domesticated because they have more flavor from eating wild herbs.

Conejo con naranja

Rabbit with Orange

2 rabbits, about 3 pounds each · 6 tablespoons oil · 1 medium onion, peeled and chopped · 1 tablespoon flour · 1 1/2 cups white wine · 3 large oranges · 1 sprig parsley, chopped · 1 bay leaf · 1 garlic clove, crushed · thyme, a pinch · 3/4 teaspoon salt · 1/4 teaspoon pepper · parsley for garnish, chopped ·

Cut the rabbits in serving pieces. Heat the oil in a Dutch oven or large pan. Fry the onion, and when it begins to brown add the rabbit pieces and brown them. Sprinkle the flour on the browned pieces; add the wine, a couple of slices of orange peel (the orange part only with no white membrane), parsley, bay leaf, garlic, thyme, salt, and pepper. Cover and cook over medium heat for 1 hour. Add the juice of 2 of the oranges; cook another 30 minutes, stirring from time to time.

Peel and slice the third orange. Place the pieces of rabbit on a serving platter. Remove the 2 slices of orange peel and bay leaf from the sauce. Pour the sauce over the rabbit and garnish the platter with the orange slices and parsley.

SERVES 6.

Conejo escabechado

Pickled Rabbit

1 rabbit, about 3 pounds · 1/2 cup oil · 3 whole garlic cloves · 2 bay leaves · 6 whole black peppers · 3/4 cup wine vinegar · 1/2 cup water · salt ·

Cut the rabbit in serving pieces. Heat the oil in a frying pan, and brown the pieces of rabbit a few at a time in the oil. As they brown, place them in a pan for marinating. The pieces should be crowded.

Leave at least 5 tablespoons of oil in the frying pan. Heat the garlic, bay leaves, and black pepper in the oil. Then remove the pan from the heat, stir in the vinegar and water. Pour the marinade over the rabbit. If it doesn't completely cover, add more water. Sprinkle with salt, cover the pan, and cook over low

164

heat for about 1 hour, or until the rabbit is tender. May be served at once, or refrigerated and served cold.

SERVES 3-4.

Conejo guisado con vino blanco

Rabbit Cooked with White Wine

2 rabbits, about 3 pounds each ·
8 tablespoons oil ·
1 medium-sized onion, finely chopped ·
1 tablespoon flour ·
3/4 cup white wine ·
1/2 cup cold water ·
thyme, a pinch ·
1/4 bay leaf, crushed · 1 sprig parsley, chopped ·
1 garlic clove, crushed ·
1/2 teaspoon salt ·
parsley for garnish ·

Cut the rabbits in serving pieces. Heat the oil in a pan and fry the onion about 5 minutes. Then brown the rabbit pieces in the oil (about 15 minutes). Sprinkle with the flour, turning to completely cover all the pieces. Add the wine, water, thyme, bay leaf, parsley, garlic, and salt. Cover the pan and cook over low heat for 45 minutes. Test for tenderness. If the rabbit is not tender, cook another 15 or 20 minutes.

Serve on a platter covering the rabbit with the sauce. Garnish the platter with parsley.

Good served with mashed potatoes.

SERVES 6.

Pierna de corzo con salsa de grosella

Leg of Deer with Currant Sauce

deer leg, about
5 pounds · 1 bay
leaf · thyme, a
pinch ·
1/4 teaspoon
nutmeg ·
1/4 teaspoon black
pepper ·
5 tablespoons oil ·
3 garlic cloves,
whole · salt and
pepper ·

Crush the bay leaf with the thyme, nutmeg, and black pepper; mix with the oil. Cover the leg of deer with this oil mixture and refrigerate at least 4 hours.

Before roasting, insert the 3 cloves of garlic deep into the meat and sprinkle with salt and pepper. The fat side should be placed up in the roasting pan. In a 325° preheated oven, roast the meat. Allow 30 minutes per pound for well-done (about 2 1/2 hours for a 5 pound leg). Baste frequently, and add a cup of water after 1 1/2 hours of roasting time.

FOR THE SAUCE:
1/2 cup red currant
jelly · 1/4 cup red
wine · 1/2 teaspoon
dry mustard ·
1/4 cup cognac ·
2 tablespoons olive
oil · 1 tablespoon
lemon juice ·

For the sauce, mix all of the ingredients together, breaking up the jelly with a fork. You may prefer to mix the sauce in a blender or food processor.

Carve the meat like a leg of lamb and serve on a platter. Serve the sauce in a separate dish.

SERVES 8-10.

166

los legumbres y las ensaladas

10

vegetables and salads

Vegetables are plentiful and enjoyed by the native Spaniards. Spain and the United States share the same vegetables, but the manner in which they are prepared and served is entirely different in both countries. With the exception of potatoes, vegetables in Spain are usually served as a separate course, frequently the first course, and may be mixed with other vegetables or meat.

Fresh fruit is available everywhere in Spain and often substituted for salad. If salad is ordered in a restaurant, it undoubtedly will be a green salad served with oil and vinegar.

Thanks to my neighbor, Mildred Ruff, I would like to share with you some of the vegetable and salad dishes that appeared on a buffet table at the Hotel Tres Reyes during her recent trip to Pamplona, Spain.

The center of the table was adorned with a huge bowl on a pedestal filled with every type of fresh fruit; tomatoes were sliced thick garnished with ripe olives and sprinkled with olive oil, mounds of tuna fish salad with pickles, artichokes with capers and sauce, green peas with sauce, large white fresh asparagus, green beans vinaigrette, artichoke hearts cooked with meat and seasoning, gelatin with mussels, and the very famous cold tomato soup—gazpacho with croutons, sliced

tomatoes, cucumbers and bell pepper. (Even though gazpacho is technically a soup, it could be substituted for a salad.)

Other unusual salads, or salad substitutions, which may not sound out-of-the-ordinary but were in their preparation included: chickpea salad, tomatoes stuffed with seafood, curried eggs topped with swirled anchovies surrounded by black olives, cornucopias filled with macaroni salad, mushrooms and onions vinaigrette, chicken salad surrounded by very thin alternating slices of tomato and lemon or carrot and cucumber. Also on the table were potato salad with poppy seeds and lots of Spanish mayonnaise, chopped tomatoes and small white onions with cubed potatoes sprinkled with olive oil; and on a bed of lettuce, hard-boiled eggs stuffed with salmon but turned salmon-side down and covered with sauce.

Alcachofas con vinagreta

Artichokes with Vinaigrette Sauce

12 small artichokes, or 2 frozen packages · 1 teaspoon salt · 3 tablespoons olive oil ·

FOR THE SAUCE: 1 teaspoon salt · 1/4 teaspoon pepper · 3/4 teaspoon paprika · 1 1/2 teaspoon dry mustard · 1 1/2 teaspoons sugar · oregano, a pinch · 1/3 cup olive oil · 1/4 cup vinegar · juice of 1 lemon ·

Wash the artichokes under running water. Remove the outside leaves and trim the stem. Put them in a pan with enough water to cover along with the salt and olive oil. Bring to a boil; lower the heat to medium and cook 30 minutes or until tender. Drain upside down. For the frozen artichokes, follow the directions on the package but do add the olive oil to the water.

For the sauce, combine salt, pepper, paprika, dry mustard, sugar and oregano in a pan. Add olive oil, vinegar, and lemon juice. Bring to a boil and serve hot in 6 individual dishes.

SERVES 6.

Esparragos verdes en salsa

Green Asparagus in Sauce

2 pounds fresh asparagus · salt ·

FOR THE SAUCE: 3 tablespoons flour · 3 tablespoons olive oil · 1/4 teaspoon salt · 1/2 teaspoon dry mustard · 3/4 cup milk · 3/4 cup half-and-half · 1/3 cup Cheddar cheese, grated ·

Wash asparagus under running water. Cut tips from lower stalks. Cook the stalks in enough salted boiling water to cover for 15 minutes; add tips and cook 5 more minutes.

In a small saucepan, blend the flour in the oil; add salt and mustard. Over low heat, gradually stir in the milk and cream. Stir to blend; then add cheese and stir continually until the mixture is thick and smooth.

Serve the sauce in a separate dish.

SERVES 6.

170

Fabada

Bean Stew

Here is one version of FABADA, which was made famous in the area of Asturias.

1 pound dried butter beans · salt · 1/4 cup olive oil · 1 medium-sized onion, chopped · 2 cloves garlic, crushed · 1/2 pound ham, cubed · 1/4 pound bacon, sliced · 2 cups tomato purée · 1 teaspoon salt · 1/2 teaspoon paprika · 6 slices chorizo sausage, or substitute pepperoni ·

Soak the beans overnight in cold water. Cook them the next day in enough water to cover to which salt has been added. More water will have to be added as they cook. Follow the directions on the package in cooking them until they are tender. Drain.

Heat the olive oil in a frying pan. Fry the onion and garlic for a few minutes; then add the ham and bacon; brown. Add tomato, salt, and paprika.

Put the beans, tomato mixture, and sausage in an oven-proof casserole. Mix well; cover and cook at 350° for 30 minutes.

SERVES 6.

Verduras a la española

Spanish-style Beans

1/4 cup olive oil · 1/2 cup onion, chopped · 1 garlic clove, crushed · 1 cup lima beans, cooked or canned · 2 cups cut green beans, cooked or canned · 3 medium-sized tomatoes, peeled and chopped · 2 tablespoons parsley, minced · salt, to taste ·

Heat the oil in a frying pan; sauté onion and garlic until tender. Add lima beans, green beans, tomatoes, parsley, and salt to taste. Bring to a boil; lower heat and simmer 15 minutes.

To prepare fresh lima beans, shell and wash the beans. Cook covered in a very small amount of boiling salted water for 20 to 30 minutes.

To prepare fresh green beans, remove ends and strings. Snap in 1-inch pieces. Cook covered in a small amount of boiled salted water for 20 to 30 minutes.

SERVES 4.

Habas a la andaluza

Andalusian-style Lima Beans

2 cups lima beans, fresh or dried · 2 tablespoons butter · 1/4 pound ham, cut in strips · 2 cups tomatoes, canned or peeled and chopped if fresh · 1 bay leaf · 1/2 teaspoon salt · 1/4 teaspoon black pepper · 1/4 teaspoon paprika ·

For fresh lima beans, shell and wash the beans. Cook covered in a small amount of boiling salted water for 20-30 minutes.

Dried limas should be soaked overnight in 6 cups of water. Cook covered, in the water in which the beans soaked, for 2 to 3 hours. Salt should be added after 30 minutes of cooking time.

Drain the beans. Melt the butter in a frying pan; then add ham, tomatoes, bay leaf, salt, pepper, and paprika. Simmer 15 minutes. Add beans; cook 5 more minutes mixing well. Remove bay leaf and serve at once.

SERVES 6.

Judías verdes a la castellana

Castilian-style Green Beans

2 1/2 to 3 cups cooked or canned whole green beans · 3 tablespoons olive oil · 1/4 cup pimientos, chopped · 1 clove garlic, chopped · 1 tablespoon parsley, chopped · 1/2 teaspoon salt · dash of pepper ·

To prepare the fresh beans, remove ends and strings. Leave whole, and cook in a small amount of boiling water, to which salt has been added, for 20 to 30 minutes or until the beans are tender. Drain.

Heat the oil in a pan. Fry the pimientos, garlic, and parsley in the oil for several minutes. Season with salt and pepper. Mix the beans with the pimiento mixture and serve at once.

SERVES 6.

Zanahorias en salsa

Carrots in Sauce

You may have noticed how often carrots are combined with other dishes. Seldom are carrots served alone, but here is a way of preparing carrots that I think you will find delicious.

1 1/2 pounds carrots · 1/4 cup olive oil · 1 medium onion, peeled and sliced · 2 tablespoons flour · 3/4 cup white wine · 1 tablespoon parsley, chopped · 1/2 teaspoon salt ·

Wash and scrape the carrots. Slice; or leave whole if young carrots. Cook, covered in small amount of salted water from 25 to 30 minutes, or until tender. Young carrots should be tender in 15 to 20 minutes. Drain.

Heat the oil in a pan; add the onion and fry over medium heat about 6 minutes. Blend in the flour; then slowly add the wine and enough water to make a medium sauce. Add parsley, salt, and the carrots. Cook over low heat about 15 minutes, mixing the sauce with the carrots.

SERVES 6.

Zanahorias glaseadas

Glazed Carrots

1/2 pound baby carrots, or large carrots cut in strips · 1/4 cup butter · sugar ·

Wash and scrape the carrots. Cook, covered in small amount of salted water about 15 minutes, or until tender. Drain on paper towels.

Melt the butter in a heavy skillet. Roll the carrots in sugar and simmer in the butter until glazed, turning frequently.

SERVES 4-6.

Coliflor con salsa de vinagreta

Cauliflower Vinaigrette

1 medium-sized head cauliflower ·

FOR THE SAUCE:
2 tablespoons vinegar · 6 tablespoons olive oil · 1 tablespoon parsley, chopped · 1 tablespoon onion, finely chopped · 1/4 teaspoon salt ·

Remove leaves and stem of cauliflower. Separate into flowerets and cook in boiling water about 10 to 15 minutes.

Prepare the sauce by mixing the vinegar, oil, parsley, onion, and salt in a blender or food processor.

Pour over the flowerets of cauliflower and serve hot, or marinate in the refrigerator for several hours and serve cold.

SERVES 6.

Coliflor fría con mayonesa

Cold Cauliflower with Mayonnaise

1 medium-sized head cauliflower · 1 teaspoon salt ·

Remove leaves and stem of cauliflower. Separate into flowerets and cook in boiling water, to which the teaspoon of salt has been added, about 10 to 15 minutes. Drain and refrigerate.

174

FOR THE
MAYONNAISE:
2 egg yolks ·
1 teaspoon salt ·
1/2 teaspoon dry
mustard · 1 cup
olive oil · juice of
1 lemon ·
2 hard-boiled
eggs ·

Prepare the mayonnaise by mixing the room-temperature egg yolks, salt, and mustard in an electric mixer or blender at lowest speed. Add olive oil drop by drop at first. As the mixture begins to thicken, add the oil in a thin stream. Blend in the lemon juice and refrigerate.

To serve, place the cold flowerets in a vegetable dish; cover them with the mayonnaise and garnish with sliced hard-boiled eggs.

SERVES 6.

Garbanzos refritos

Refried Chickpeas

1/2 pound
chickpeas ·
1 teaspoon baking
soda · 1 teaspoon
salt · 4 tablespoons
oil ·
1 medium-sized
onion, peeled and
chopped · 1 garlic
clove, crushed ·
3 medium-sized
tomatoes, peeled
and chopped ·
1/4 pound summer
sausage, thinly
sliced (or
substitute
1/4 pound cooked
ham, chopped) ·
1/2 teaspoon
paprika ·

Soak the chickpeas in water, to which soda and salt have been added, overnight or at least 12 hours before cooking. Drain.

Cook the chickpeas in a pot with water above the level of the chickpeas. More water probably will have to be added as they cook. The time for cooking will depend on the chickpeas. Instructions should be on the package, but they should boil gently for several hours (2 to 4).

Heat the oil in a Dutch oven or large pan; sauté the onion and garlic for about 5 minutes. Add tomatoes and cook another 10 minutes, mashing them as they cook. Add the sausage (or ham), paprika, salt, and chickpeas. Heat thoroughly for 5 minutes or more and serve hot.

SERVES 6.

175

Berenjenas a la española

Spanish-style Eggplant

1/3 cup olive oil ·
1 large onion,
sliced in rings ·
2 garlic cloves,
crushed ·
4 medium-sized
eggplants, peeled
and diced · 1 green
pepper, seeds
removed and sliced
in rings ·
4 medium-sized
tomatoes,
quartered ·
2 teaspoons salt ·
1/2 teaspoon
pepper · 1/2 cup
ripe olives ·

Heat the oil in a large frying pan; sauté onion and garlic about 5 minutes. Then add eggplant, green pepper, tomatoes, salt, and pepper. Sauté about 30 minutes or until the vegetables are tender.

Serve hot, garnishing the platter with olives. May also be refrigerated for days and served either hot or cold.

SERVES 8-10.

Berenjenas rellanas

Stuffed Eggplant

6 small eggplants ·
1/2 pound
mushrooms ·
2 tablespoons
butter · juice of
1/2 lemon ·
1/4 teaspoon salt ·
5 tablespoons olive
oil ·
1 medium-sized
onion, peeled and
chopped ·
4 tablespoons flour ·
1 teaspoon salt ·
2 cups cold milk ·

Remove the stem; cut a slice out of each eggplant. Scoop out but reserve the pulp, leaving about 1/2 inch of the eggplant in the shell.

Clean and slice the mushrooms; then sauté them in butter, lemon juice, and salt over low heat for 10 minutes.

In another pan heat 3 tablespoons of the olive oil, and sauté the onion and the pulp from the eggplant; cook until tender.

When the mushrooms are cooked, set them aside. Prepare a béchamel sauce by measuring the butter in the pan and adding enough to measure 2 tablespoons

176

1 egg yolk, beaten ·
1/2 cup Gruyère or
other white cheese

plus 2 tablespoons of oil. Blend in the flour and salt. Remove from the heat, gradually stirring in the milk. Return to the heat; add the egg yolk and stir constantly until the sauce is smooth. Add the mushrooms, onion, and eggplant pulp. Mix well.

Place the eggplant shells in a well-oiled casserole dish. Stuff them with the mushroom mixture. Top with the cheese.

Bake in a 350° oven for 30 minutes.

SERVES 6.

Patatas al horno

Baked Potatoes

6 large baking
potatoes · water ·
1 teaspoon salt ·
1/4 cup olive oil ·

Peel the potatoes; cover them with water and add salt. Let stand 10 minutes; then drain and dry with paper towels. Place in a baking dish and pour the oil over the potatoes, turning to coat on all sides.

Bake in a 350° preheated oven for 2 hours, turning the potatoes after the first hour.

SERVES 6.

177

Tortas de patatas con queso

Cheese Potato Cakes

2 cups raw potatoes, grated · ice water · 1/2 cup onion, chopped · 2 tablespoons olive oil · 1/4 cup Cheddar cheese, grated · 1 egg, slightly beaten · 1/4 teaspoon salt · 1/8 teaspoon pepper · 1/4 cup olive oil ·

Grate the potatoes using a hand grater or electric food processor. Place grated potatoes in ice water for 5 minutes. Drain and dry on paper towels. Sauté onion in 2 tablespoons of olive oil until tender. Mix the onion with the potatoes, cheese, egg, salt, and pepper.

Heat the 1/4 cup olive oil in a frying pan. Scoop up the potato mixture using a 1/4 cup measure, and fry in hot oil. When cakes are brown on one side, turn and brown on other side. Several may be fried at the same time. Drain on paper towels and serve hot.

SERVES 4 OR MORE (8 CAKES).

Patatas a la vasca

Basque-style Potatoes

2 pounds potatoes · ice water · 1 tablespoon butter · 1/2 cup onion, chopped · 1 garlic clove, minced · 1/2 cup celery, chopped · 1/2 cup carrots, grated · 2 beef bouillon cubes · 2 cups boiling water · 1 teaspoon salt · 2 tablespoons parsley, chopped ·

Peel the potatoes and cut them in 1-inch cubes. Place them in enough ice water to cover and set aside.

Melt the butter in a 10-inch frying pan. Add onion, garlic, celery, and carrots; cook over low heat until the vegetables are tender. Drain the potatoes, and stir into vegetable mixture.

Dissolve bouillon cubes in boiling water. Add bouillon broth to potato mixture; salt and bring to a boil. Reduce heat; cover the pan and simmer 25 minutes or until the potatoes are tender. Place in a serving dish. Top with the chopped parsley and serve hot.

SERVES 6.

Guisantes sencillos

Simple Peas

3 pounds peas in pod · 3 tablespoons oil · 2 small onions, peeled but left whole · 1 cup water · 1 teaspoon sugar · 1 tablespoon parsley, finely chopped · 1/2 teaspoon salt · 1/4 teaspoon pepper · 1/2 cup cooked ham, diced ·

Shell the peas. Heat the oil in a pan; put the whole onions in the pan, and cook over medium heat about 3 or 4 minutes, without browning them. Add the peas; let them cook in the oil a minute or two. Then add water, sugar, parsley, salt, and pepper. Bring to a boil; lower the heat to low and cook 10 minutes. Add ham and cook another 10 minutes or until the peas are tender.

SERVES 6.

Manera de preparar y cocer las espinacas

Way of Preparing and Cooking Spinach

Discard the roots and tough stems of the spinach leaves. Wash the leaves under running water, or through several clean, cold waters, lifting the leaves out of the water each time.

Cook covered over medium heat in a heavy pan. Do not add water but 1 teaspoon of salt for every 2 pounds of spinach. Turn with fork frequently, and cook 8 to 10 minutes. Add lemon juice and butter before serving.

ALLOW 2 POUNDS OF SPINACH FOR 6 SERVINGS.

Crema de espinacas

Creamed Spinach

2 to 2 1/2 pounds spinach · 1 tablespoon butter · 2 tablespoons oil · 2 tablespoons flour · 1 teaspoon salt · 1 cup cold milk · 2 hard-boiled eggs, quartered ·

Prepare the spinach according to the preceding instructions, "Way of Preparing and Cooking Spinach." Drain.

Prepare the sauce by melting the butter with the oil; blend in the flour and salt. Remove from heat and gradually stir in the milk. Return to heat; stir constantly until the sauce is smooth. Add the spinach to the sauce and mix well for several minutes.

Serve hot, garnishing the dish with the pieces of hard-boiled egg.

SERVES 6.

Calabaza frita

Fried Yellow Squash

4 1/2 cups yellow squash, unpeeled, cut 1/4 inch thick · 1/4 cup olive oil · 1 teaspoon basil · 2 teaspoons sugar · 1 teaspoon salt · 1/4 teaspoon pepper ·

Heat the oil in a large frying pan. Sauté the squash with the basil, sugar, salt, and pepper until tender, about 15 to 20 minutes. Stir frequently.

SERVES 6.

Calabaza frita (zucchini)

Fried Zucchini

4 to 4 1/2 cups
zucchini, cut about
1/4 inch thick ·
1/4 cup olive oil ·
1 teaspoon oregano ·
2 teaspoons sugar ·
1 teaspoon salt ·
1/4 teaspoon
pepper ·

Heat the oil in a large frying pan. Sauté the zucchini with the oregano, sugar, salt, and pepper until tender, about 15 to 20 minutes. Stir frequently.

SERVES 6.

Migas sazonadas

Seasoned Crumbs

Here is an extra touch that can be added to hot cooked vegetables and is excellent with salads.

2 cups fresh bread
crumbs ·
2 tablespoons olive
oil · 1 teaspoon
paprika ·
1/2 teaspoon salt ·
1/8 teaspoon
pepper ·

Sauté crumbs in the oil over low heat until golden brown, about 10 minutes, stirring frequently. Stir in paprika, salt, and pepper. Cool to room temperature. Serve over hot vegetables.

MAKES 2 CUPS.

VEGETABLE SALADS
Legumbres marinados

Marinated Vegetables

2 cups cooked vegetables · 1/2 cup of either: oil and vinegar dressing, vinaigrette sauce, white wine salad dressing · leaves of lettuce ·

You may choose from a variety of vegetables like peas, green beans, baby lima beans, flowerets of cauliflower, and carrots.

Cook the vegetables until just done. Combine with the 1/2 cup of marinade. Refrigerate for several hours, turning the vegetables occasionally.

Serve the vegetables mixed together on beds of lettuce, or separated in individual bowls on a Lazy Susan.

SERVES 4.

Oil and Vinegar Dressing

2/3 cup olive oil · 1/3 cup vinegar · 1 teaspoon sugar · 1 teaspoon salt · 1/4 teaspoon pepper ·

Shake the ingredients together in a jar, or blend at slowest speed in an electric blender. Do not refrigerate.

MAKES 1 CUP.

Vinaigrette Sauce

1 small onion, peeled and finely chopped · 1 tablespoon parsley, minced · 1 garlic clove · 1/2 teaspoon salt · 1 cup olive oil · 1/3 cup wine vinegar ·

Combine onion, parsley, whole garlic clove, salt, and oil. Let stand at room temperature for 30 minutes. Discard garlic clove. Add vinegar and shake well.

MAKES 1 1/3 CUPS.

White Wine Salad Dressing

3/4 cup dry white wine · 1/2 cup olive oil · 1/4 cup white vinegar · 1/4 cup onion, finely chopped · 1/2 garlic clove, crushed · 1 teaspoon salt · 1/4 teaspoon pepper ·

Blend all ingredients by shaking well in a jar, or mixing in an electric blender or food processor.

MAKES 1 3/4 CUPS.

Ensalada de tres clases de judías

Three Bean Salad

1 can green beans (1 lb. size) · 1 can wax beans (1 lb. size) · 1 can kidney beans (1 lb. size) · oil and vinegar dressing ·

Drain the liquid from the cans and combine the beans.

Double the "Oil and Vinegar Dressing" recipe on page 182. Mix the beans with the dressing. Chill for several hours before serving.

SERVES 12-16.

Esparragos a la vinagretta

Asparagus Vinaigrette

1 pound fresh asparagus · salt · vinaigrette sauce ·

Wash asparagus under running water; cut off tough white ends. Cook stalk side down but with the tips out of the water in as deep a pan as possible in boiling salted water. Cook the stalks about 12 minutes; then put the tip side down and cook another 4 minutes.

Drain and cover with Vinaigrette Sauce (page 182). Refrigerate for several hours before serving.

SERVES 4.

Ensalada de maíz y pimiento

Corn and Pimiento Salad

1 3/4 cups canned whole kernel corn, drained · 1/4 cup pimientos, diced ·

FOR THE MARINADE: 2/3 cup olive oil · 1/3 cup vinegar · 1 teaspoon sugar · 1 teaspoon dill weed · 1 teaspoon salt · 1/4 teaspoon pepper ·

Mix the corn and pimientos together. Shake all ingredients for the marinade in a jar, or mix in an electric blender or food processor.

Pour the marinade over the corn and pimiento mixture. Chill for several hours before serving.

SERVES 4.

Ensalada de tomates marinados

Marinated Tomato Salad

3 medium-sized tomatoes, sliced · 2 small onions, thinly sliced · 1/2 cup oil and vinegar dressing (page 182) · 2 tablespoons parsley, chopped ·

Combine the slices of tomatoes and onions. Pour the dressing over them and refrigerate for 2 hours or more. Sprinkle with parsley before serving.

SERVES 4.

Ensalada de pimientos y tomates

Tomato and Pepper Salad

FOR THE DRESSING:
2/3 cup olive oil ·
1/2 cup vinegar ·
1 garlic clove,
whole · 1 teaspoon
sugar · 1 teaspoon
salt · 1/4 teaspoon
pepper ·

4 medium-sized
tomatoes · 1 large
or 2 small red or
green peppers, cut
in strips · lettuce ·

Prepare the dressing the day before it is to be used by shaking all of the ingredients together in a jar. Store at room temperature, and remove clove of garlic before serving.

Combine the tomato slices with the pepper strips. Place on leaves of lettuce. Pour the dressing over them, or serve the dressing as a side dish.

Also good served with seasoned crumbs (see page 181).

SERVES 4.

Ensalada Isabella

Isabel-style Potato Salad

2 1/2-3 cups cooked
potatoes, cubed or
sliced · 1/2 cup
celery, sliced ·
4 apples, cored,
peeled and sliced ·

FOR THE
MAYONNAISE:
1 clove garlic,
crushed ·
1/2 teaspoon salt ·
1/4 teaspoon
pepper ·
1/4 teaspoon dry
mustard · 1 egg
yolk · 1 cup olive
oil · 1 tablespoon
lemon juice ·

Mix the potatoes, celery, and apples together.

For the mayonnaise, put the garlic, salt, pepper, mustard, and egg yolk in a blender and mix well. Add the oil a few drops at a time until the mixture is thick, then stir in the lemon juice.

Mix the mayonnaise with the potatoes, celery, and apples. Refrigerate before serving.

SERVES 4.

Ensalada española de naranjas

Spanish-style Orange Salad

lettuce · 2 oranges, peeled and sliced · 2 medium-sized onions, thinly sliced · 1 small green pepper, thinly sliced · 2 pimientos, drained and chopped · white wine salad dressing ·

Line the salad bowl with leaves of lettuce. Arrange the slices of orange, onion, green pepper, and pimientos in an attractive design on top of the lettuce. Refrigerate.

Prepare the white wine salad dressing according to the recipe on page 183.

Before serving, pour the dressing over the salad and serve immediately.

SERVES 4.

Ensalada con salsa de legumbres

Tossed Salad with Vegetable Dressing

FOR THE DRESSING: 1 large carrot, chopped · 1 large onion, chopped · 1 celery stalk, chopped · 1 garlic clove, crushed · 1 teaspoon pepper · 2 tablespoons wine vinegar · 1 egg · 1 cup olive oil ·

1 head lettuce · 3 tomatoes, cut in wedges · 1 cucumber, sliced · 2 hard-boiled eggs, quartered ·

Prepare the dressing at least one day before it is to be used by placing the carrot, onion, celery, garlic, pepper, wine, and egg in an electric blender or food processor. Turn on and off rapidly until the vegetables are puréed. Turn to high speed and add olive oil in a thin stream. Store in a jar with a lid in the refrigerator.

Break up the head of lettuce in a salad bowl and combine with tomatoes and cucumber. You may prefer other combinations, but remember the dressing contains vegetables. Toss the salad with the dressing. Garnish the bowl with the eggs before serving.

SERVES 6.

Ensalada a la valenciana

Valencia-style Chef Salad

FOR THE SAUCE:
3 tablespoons onion, chopped ·
1 tablespoon parsley, minced ·
1/2 teaspoon salt ·
1 garlic clove, whole · 1 cup olive oil · 1/3 cup wine vinegar ·

3 cups cooked rice ·
1/2 green pepper, chopped ·
1 pimiento, diced ·
1 cup chopped of cooked ham, veal, turkey, chicken or other left-over meat ·

1 1/2 cup olives, black or green ·
2 small tomatoes, cut in wedges ·
3 hard-boiled eggs, quartered ·
lettuce ·

To make the sauce combine the onion, parsley, salt, whole garlic clove, and oil. Let stand 30 minutes. Discard the clove of garlic; add vinegar and stir well.

Cook the rice according to the instructions on the package. Combine the rice with the green pepper, pimiento, and meat. Toss with 1/3 cup of the sauce. Chill.

Marinate the olives and tomatoes in the remaining sauce.

Place leaves of lettuce on a platter. Arrange the rice mixture over the lettuce, and place the olives, tomatoes, and egg wedges around the edge of the platter. Pour the sauce in which the olives and tomatoes marinated over the rice mixture and serve chilled.

Serve with French bread for a complete meal.

SERVES 4-6.

Ensalada de frutas

Fruit Salad

FOR THE DRESSING:
1/2 cup olive oil ·
2 garlic cloves,
quartered ·
1 medium onion,
sliced · 1/2 cup
apple sauce ·
1/4 cup vinegar ·
1 teaspoon salt ·
1/8 teaspoon
pepper ·

5 red apples, cores
removed and cut in
cubes · 1/2 cup
celery · 1/2 cup
seedless grapes ·
1/2 cup pineapple
tidbits · 1/3 cup
walnut pieces ·

Combine olive oil with garlic and onion. Leave at room temperature for 3 hours. Remove garlic and onion; then mix in apple sauce, vinegar, salt and pepper.

Mix apples, celery, grapes, pineapple, and nuts. Blend in the dressing and chill before serving.

SERVES 6.

los postres
11
desserts

Spanish desserts and sweets resemble those that are popular today in Mexico, for sweets were not known in the New World until the Spanish arrived. It was the Spanish nuns in Mexico who prepared desserts and fancy candies for gifts or to be sold. Even today in Spain, one can purchase pastries and sweets made in the convents. Sweets were not native to the Spaniards either, but were introduced by the Moors, who inhabited the peninsula from 711 until 1492.

When looking at a menu in a Spanish restaurant, it might be assumed that Spaniards do not like sweets, but this is not true. There are many pastry shops in Spain, but heavier desserts, like cake for example, are eaten in the late afternoon as a snack several hours before the late meal at night. After a multi-course meal, any of a number of fresh fruits may be enjoyed. Sometimes cheese is served for dessert.

Flan, a type of caramel custard presented in many different ways, is the most popular dessert in Spain today.

Flan al caramelo

Spanish Caramel Custard

2 cups sugar ·
~~**1/2 cup water**~~ ·
1 quart milk ·
8 eggs · 1 teaspoon vanilla ·
1/2 teaspoon salt ·

In a heavy saucepan or skillet over low heat, stir 1 cup of the sugar with the ~~1/2 cup of water~~ until the sugar dissolves. Continue to cook without stirring until the sugar turns into a golden syrup. Pour into a flan pan or a round 2-quart baking dish. Tilt to coat bottom and sides; let cool for at least 30 minutes.

Heat the milk until lukewarm. In a large bowl beat the room-temperature eggs together with the remaining 1 cup of sugar, vanilla, salt, and 1 cup of the lukewarm milk. Blend well; then add the remaining lukewarm milk and beat to blend. Pour through a sieve on top of the syrup.

In a 350° preheated oven place pan in a larger pan that contains 1 inch of hot water. Bake about 40 to 50 minutes, or until a silver knife inserted in the center comes out clean. *up to 1 hr 15 min*

Cool; then cover and refrigerate about 8 hours. Unmold by running a knife around the rim; place serving plate over pan. Turn pan over to serve.

SERVES 12.

Flan al ron

Rum Custard

1 3/4 cup sugar ·
1 tablespoon
water · 2 cups
half-and-half ·
2 cups milk ·
4 whole eggs ·
4 egg yolks ·
2 tablespoons dark
rum · 1/2 teaspoon
salt ·

Carmelize the sugar by placing 1 cup of the sugar in a skillet over low heat. When sugar begins to form a syrup, add water and stir constantly with a wooden spoon until the sugar is melted and smooth. When the sugar turns a golden color, pour into a flan pan or a round 2-quart baking dish. Rotate to coat bottom and sides; set aside to cool at least 30 minutes.

Heat half-and-half with the milk until lukewarm. In a large bowl beat the eggs and egg yolks with the remaining 3/4 cup sugar until the sugar dissolves. Add cream, milk, rum, and salt. Stir to blend, and pour through a sieve on top of the syrup.

In a 350° preheated oven place baking dish in a larger pan that contains 1 inch of water. Cover baking dish with foil. Reduce heat to 325° and bake about 2 hours, or until a silver knife inserted in center of custard comes out clean.

Cool; then cover and refrigerate overnight, if possible. Unmold by running a knife around the rim; invert dish onto serving platter. Refrigerate until ready to serve.

SERVES 8-10.

Flan con peras

Pear Custard

Prepare the pears by cutting 5 pears in half lengthwise, removing the core, and cooking in boiling water for 20 minutes. Chop in bite-size pieces. Follow the recipe for "Spanish Caramel Custard." Place the pears over the carmelized sugar in the baking pan; add custard and bake as directed.

Flan de coco

Coconut Custard

Follow the recipe for "Spanish Caramel Custard," on page 191. Add 1 cup of shredded coconut over the carmelized sugar in the baking pan; add custard and bake according to the directions.

Bizcocho

Spongecake

5 eggs, separated ·
1/4 teaspoon salt ·
1 cup sugar ·
1 teaspoon lemon
rind, grated ·
1 tablespoon lemon
juice · 1 cup flour,
sifted ·
1/2 teaspoon
baking powder ·
powdered sugar ·

Beat egg whites nearly stiff. Add salt and continue to beat until batter will form peaks. Slowly beat in the sugar, adding a little at a time and beating after each addition.

Beat the egg yolks until thick; add lemon rind and juice. When mixture is quite thick, fold in beaten egg whites. Sift the baking powder with the flour, and gradually fold into the egg mixture.

Pour into a lightly greased tube pan. Bake in a 325° preheated oven from 50 minutes to an hour. Cake should spring back when lightly touched. Invert pan; allow to cool before removing from pan. Sprinkle with powdered sugar and serve.

Bizcocho con mantequilla

Butter Spongecake

Follow the preceding recipe for "Spongecake" adding 1/4 cup of melted, but not hot, butter after the addition of the flour. Bake as directed in a 325° oven from 50 minutes to an hour.

Bizcocho borracho

Drunken Spongecake

4 tablespoons sugar ·
4 tablespoons
water · 1/2 cup
brandy, or
substitute rum ·
3/4 cup powdered
(confectioners)
sugar · hot water ·
1/2 pint whipping
cream ·
1 tablespoon
sugar · fresh
strawberries, or
other fresh fruit ·

Bake the spongecake following the directions for "Spongecake" on page 193 and allow to cool; then place on a cake plate.

Bring the sugar and water to a boil, and boil for 5 minutes. Pour the syrup over the cake; then sprinkle with the brandy or rum. Mix the powdered sugar with a little hot water until it can be spread easily. Ice the top of the cake. Whip the cream, adding the sugar. Place in the center of the cake, and decorate with the strawberries or other fresh seasonal fruit.

Torta de chocolate

Chocolate Fleck Cake

2 1/4 cups cake
flour · 1 3/4 cups
sugar · 3 teaspoons
baking powder ·
1 teaspoon salt ·
1/2 cup olive oil ·
5 egg yolks ·
3/4 cup cold water ·
2 teaspoons vanilla ·
1 cup egg whites ·
1/2 teaspoon cream
of tartar · 3 squares
unsweetened
chocolate, grated ·

Sift the cake flour with the sugar, baking powder, and salt into a mixing bowl. Make a "well" in the center; add the oil, egg yolks, water, and vanilla to the well. Beat until smooth by hand or at lowest speed with a mixer.

Beat egg whites with cream of tartar until stiff. Fold in flour mixture, then the grated chocolate. Pour into an ungreased tube pan.

Bake in a 325° preheated oven for 50 minutes. Raise the heat to 350° and continue baking about 15 minutes more or until cake springs back when lightly touched. Invert pan; allow to cool thoroughly. Loosen sides of pan with knife and invert onto cake plate.

Torta de pasas y nueces

Raisin Nut Cake

1 cup boiling water ·
1 cup raisins ·
1 1/2 teaspoons
baking soda ·
3 cups all-purpose
flour · 1 teaspoon
salt · 3 eggs ·
2 cups sugar ·
1 cup olive oil ·
2 teaspoons rum or
rum extract · 1 cup
walnuts or pecans,
chopped ·

Pour boiling water over raisins. Let stand 5 minutes. Stir in the baking soda. Sift the flour with the salt. Beat the eggs with the sugar; then beat the olive oil and rum into the egg and sugar mixture. Stir in the flour and fold in the nuts. Pour into a greased and lightly floured Bundt pan or a tube pan.

Bake in 350° preheated oven for 1 hour. Cool at least 15 minutes before removing to serving plate. Loosen sides of pan with knife and invert to serve. May be served warm or cold.

Torta de almendras

Almond Cake

3 eggs · 2/3 cup
sugar · 2 cups
almonds, blanched
and ground ·
1/2 cup cake flour ·
1/4 teaspoon salt ·
whipped cream ·

Beat eggs with sugar until thick. Grind the almonds in an electric blender or food processor. Mix 3/4 cups of the almonds with cake flour and salt; add to egg mixture and stir to blend. Pour into a greased and floured Bundt or tube pan.

Bake in 400° preheated oven 25 or 30 minutes. Cake is done when toothpick inserted in the middle comes out clean. Invert and cool cake. Remove to serving plate. Top each serving with whipped cream and the remaining ground almonds.

Torta de jengibre

Gingerbread Cake

2 cups apple sauce ·
1 cup dark
molasses ·
1/2 teaspoon
baking soda ·
3 cups all-purpose
flour · 2 teaspoons
baking powder ·
1/2 teaspoon salt ·
2 teaspoons ginger ·
1 1/2 teaspoons
cinnamon ·
1/2 teaspoon cloves ·
4 eggs ·
1 1/3 cups sugar ·
2/3 cup olive oil ·
1 cup walnuts or
pecans, chopped ·

Bring apple sauce to a boil. Stir in molasses and soda; cool to room temperature. Sift the flour with the baking powder, salt, ginger, cinnamon, and cloves. Set aside.

Beat the eggs until they are light in color. Gradually beat in sugar and continue beating until thick. Gradually add the oil. Add flour mixture alternately with apple sauce mixture. Fold in nuts. Pour into greased tube pan.

Bake in a 325° preheated oven for 1 hour or until a toothpick inserted in the center comes out clean. Cool about 15 minutes before removing from pan.

May be served plain or topped with whipped cream or warm apple sauce.

Crema de chocolate

Chocolate Creams

1 cup sugar · 1 cup
water · 6 egg yolks,
beaten · 1/2 cup
chocolate squares,
melted ·

Boil the sugar and water together until a thick syrup. Cool; add to beaten egg yolks. Pour into individual ovenproof dishes. Bake in a 300° preheated oven for about 45 minutes or until set. Let the creams cool a little; then pour the chocolate over the creams. Refrigerate before serving.

Crema de café

Coffee Creams

1 tablespoon unflavored gelatine · 3 eggs · 2 cups milk · 1/4 cup sugar · 4 teaspoons instant coffee · whipped cream (optional) ·

Dissolve the gelatine in a little warm water. Beat the eggs slightly; mix with the milk and sugar. Cook over low heat until the mixture begins to thicken. Mix the coffee with a little water. Add it and the gelatine to the custard. Pour in a glass dish or individual dishes and refrigerate to set.

To serve, top each serving with a scoop of whipped cream, if you desire.

Crema de coco

Coconut Cream

1/2 cup sugar · 2 tablespoons flour · 1 1/2 cups milk · 4 egg yolks · 1 teaspoon vanilla · 1/2 cup shredded coconut, chopped ·

Put the sugar and flour in the top of a double boiler. Gradually stir in the milk and continue to stir until the mixture thickens.

Beat the egg yolks; add a little of the milk mixture; then slowly add yolks to the hot mixture. Cook in the double boiler several more minutes, stirring continually. Cool; add vanilla and coconut.

May be served cold in 4 individual dishes, or excellent as a topping for sponge cake.

FRUIT COBBLERS
Tortas de fruta

Shortcake Biscuits

2 cups all-purpose flour · 3 teaspoons baking powder · 1 teaspoon salt · 3 tablespoons sugar · 7 tablespoons olive oil · about 2/3 cup milk ·

To prepare the biscuits for the shortcake, sift the flour and measure. Add baking powder, salt, and sugar. Sift again. Stir in the olive oil; add enough milk to form a soft dough.

Turn out on a lightly floured board and knead about 1/2 minute. Pat or roll out the dough until about 1/4 inch thick. Cut with floured biscuit cutter into 8 portions.

Bake as directed below.

Torta de fresas

Strawberry Shortcake

3 cups fresh strawberries, cut-up · 3/4 cup sugar · 1 tablespoon cornstarch · salt, a dash · 1 cup water · shortcake biscuits · whipped cream (optional) ·

Combine strawberries, sugar, cornstarch, salt, and water in a pan. Bring to a boil; simmer a minute or two. Pour into a 1 1/2-quart casserole. Place the shortcake biscuits on top, prepared according to the preceding recipe. Bake in a 400° preheated oven for 25 to 30 minutes. May be served hot or cold with whipped cream, if desired.

SERVES 8.

Torta de duraznos

Peach Cobbler

Substitute 3 cups of cut-up fresh peaches for the strawberries and proceed as directed for "Strawberry Shortcake" in the preceding recipe.

Torta de cerezas

Cherry Cobbler

Substitute 3 cups of fresh or canned pitted red cherries for the strawberries and proceed as directed for "Strawberry Shortcake" (page 198).

Polvorones de almendra

Almond Cookies

Polvorones, or "Mexican Wedding Cakes," are so popular in Mexico, and also in the southwestern part of the United States. Although we may think of them as Mexican, they too originated in Spain.

1/2 cup butter (do not substitute) · 1/4 cup powdered (confectioners) sugar · 1 heaping cup flour, sifted · 1/4 teaspoon salt · 1/2 teaspoon vanilla · 1 cup toasted almonds, ground · confectioners sugar for rolling ·

Cream butter; add sugar, flour, salt, vanilla, and almonds, which have been ground in an electric blender or food processor. Form into a ball and refrigerate for several hours. Then roll into balls 1 inch or more in diameter.

Bake in a 400° preheated oven about 15 minutes. Roll in the sugar while still hot; cool, and roll in the sugar again.

SERVING: 30 COOKIES OR MORE.

Arroz con leche

Rice Pudding

1 cup rice · 3 cups water · 1/2 teaspoon salt · 5 1/2 cups milk · 1 teaspoon vanilla · 1 tablespoon butter · 1 cup sugar · powdered cinnamon ·

Bring the water with the salt added to a boil. Add rice and boil for 3 minutes, stirring frequently. Drain.

Bring the milk with the vanilla added to a boil. Slowly add the rice to the boiling milk; then add butter and sugar. Boil hard about 5 minutes; reduce heat to very low, and cook covered until liquid is absorbed, 30 minutes or more. Check periodically to make sure rice doesn't burn.

Place in individual serving dishes and refrigerate for several hours. Sprinkle with cinnamon and serve cold.

SERVES 4-5.

index

English Index

202

Indice Español

207